confessions
of a bone
woman

confessions of a bone woman

realizing authentic
wildness in a civilized world

lucinda bakken white

WILD WOMAN BOOKS

WILD WOMAN BOOKS

Published by Wild Woman Books
wildwomanbooks.com

Print ISBN: 978-0-9976482-5-6
E-book ISBN: 978-0-9976482-0-1

Publisher's Cataloging-In-Publication Data
(Prepared by The Donohue Group, Inc.)

Names: White, Lucinda Bakken.

Title: Confessions of a bone woman : realizing your authentic wildness in a civilized world / Lucinda Bakken White.

Description: [Menlo Park, California] : Wild Woman Books, [2018]

Identifiers: ISBN 9780997648256 | ISBN 9780997648201 (ebook)

Subjects: LCSH: White, Lucinda Bakken. | Women—United States—Biography. | Yuppies—United States—Biography. | Women and the environment. | Women—Identity. | Self-actualization (Psychology) in women. | Dead animals. | LCGFT: Autobiographies.

Classification: LCC HQ1413.W45 .W45 2018 (print) | LCC HQ1413.W45 (ebook) | DDC 305.43/3042082092—dc23

Cover photo: Lindsy Richards/Illuminating Archetypes
Cover design: Bill Greaves/Concept West
Interior design: Kevin Callahan/BNGO Books
Tree illustrations: Sara Zieve Miller

This book is dedicated to
the animal kingdom.

With the deepest love in my heart, I will donate
25 percent of all proceeds from the sale of this book
to Earthfire Institute Wildlife Sanctuary.

contents

Chapter One

heart path

Heart path is bringing a sense of the sacred
to everyday experience.

—*Jack Kornfield*

On a warm summer day in August of 2013, I sat on a couch in
our den staring at the texture of soft padded walls covered in khaki
linen. Glancing up, I noticed the olive-green-and-gold twisted trim
set in the seams, lining the room where cloth met wooden crown
moldings and baseboard.

My husband, Rhys, and I had just returned home from dropping
our youngest off at college. The house was silent. Tired and drained, I
was in a melancholy mood, but not for the reasons you might think.

My kids were gone, and I missed them, but I missed myself just
as much. Most mothers I knew were distraught by the thought of
life after children, and they held on tightly to their kids for as long
as they could. In sharp contrast, I could hardly wait for my nest
to be empty. Barely hanging on, I was ready to let go and collapse
from depletion.

I loved being a mother, a wife, and a homemaker. But by the time
my children were teenagers, much of my joy was squelched by the
never-ending routines of meal prep, carpools, homework, housework,

volunteer work, college applications, and people pleasing. No matter how much I did, it never felt like enough, because there was always more of the same to do. Go to this party or that. Be pretty and pleasant in public. Listen to people brag about their lives and kids. Go to the gym. Wash my hair. Have sex with my husband. Walk the dog. Run errands. Put out little fires. Host extended family for dinner. Prep for the holidays. Acknowledge birthdays. Pay the bills. Organize the house. Fix what's broken. And just when I crossed the last "to do" off my list, it was time to repeat the cycle all over again.

Perhaps I could have rebounded with a month of sleep and no kids around the house, but that was not going to happen. Two of my stepsons were married with three children between them, and I was babysitting this weekend. Many women dream of and long for grandchildren. I did too. Nevertheless, I needed a breather to thoughtfully transition from being a mother to being a grandmother. In fact, I was longing to be a grandmother. Yearning to bring a sense of the sacred to the forefront of my everyday life, my heart was set on becoming a wise-woman elder with a spiritual vocation. I knew where I wanted to go; I just didn't know how to get there, and I didn't want to make a wrong turn. At a crossroads, I needed time and space to explore the deepest meaning of my heart path so I could follow, embody, and express it.

Fifteen years prior, my husband and I had realized a peak of material success and popularity that came with both blessings and burdens. I was grateful for our abundant life, but eventually the weight of living for external measures tipped me out of balance and crushed my soul.

Slowly but surely it was the animal kingdom that called me to rise from the dead. Curiously, my relationship with animals began with the touch of a bone. First I found one, and then two, followed by a burst of three, four, five, and six. When I put my hand to bone, electricity ran through my body. Enlivened, I studied the animal bones and I wondered: *To whom did they belong? What purpose did they serve? How did these animals live? And how did they die?*

In love with the bones, my heart kindled an authentically wild and burning passion that stood in stark contrast with the rest of my life. Late at night while my family slept, I researched animal anatomy, bone identification, and animal behavior. Harkening back to my ancestors, I also learned the symbolism associated with each animal and their individual parts, which enabled me to receive and interpret profound messages at every encounter.

By following my heart, I no longer felt lonely. Instead, I was deeply connected to the animal kingdom, my inner self, and a greater mysterious life-force. Looking back, I realized that bone by bone the animals I found were a metaphor for my personal process of discovering, unmasking, and reconnecting the scattered parts of my true self.

For decades I had been developing a lot of self-awareness and realizing my authentic wildness, but I was not yet fully synthesized. My soul-driven, spontaneous nature did not always align with the norms and values of the surrounding civilized culture. To protect myself, I was living a life of dichotomies, expressing different personalities with different masks in different places. All this shapeshifting of personas was depleting, and it was painful to contain or hide my full self. Terrified to come out of the closet, I was far more afraid of being trapped inside modern society's limiting and often narrow definition of what it means to be a woman, a grandmother, or an elder.

Teetering on the cusp of something old and something new, I was ripe for transformation. But change does not come easy at any time in this contemporary world, no matter how ready we are. I had a feeling that my family and friends preferred I stay the same. Few of them seemed to understand the vision born inside of me and how it was essential to my mental, emotional, physical, and spiritual well-being. After all, who dreams of being an elder?

As I sat on the couch in a slump, I noticed a flicker of movement from the corner of my eye. Shifting my view, I looked past the light streaming through a sash window and saw the orange-and-white-barred breast of a Cooper's hawk. He was perched on a post at the edge of our circular pond, looking at the lush aquatic jungle before him, full of tall fuzzy cattails; shiny-green lily pads; pink lotus blossoms; orange, black, and white koi; and iridescent dragonflies.

Animals had become my guides. They came to me often and spoke to me in symbols, the language of my soul. Intuiting a message from Hawk, I perceived that he was symbolically hunting for spiritual sustenance as represented by the fish in the water and the winged ones in flight. It was clear to me that he was suggesting I do the same to lift myself out of my funk.

Taking Hawk's advice, I decided to visit our property in the country. Just a twenty-minute drive door to door, it was another world away. The construction traffic getting out of my town was heavy as usual. My skin, neck, and back all tightened as I navigated the congestion. Everywhere I looked big trucks clogged the streets. Yards were being torn up for new construction, and the air resounded with a constant percussion of jackhammers.

Then, as I turned onto Sand Hill Road, my body softened. Heritage oaks, pines, and redwoods soothed my eyes, causing me to breathe deeply and slowly. I paid no attention to the lineup of iconic Silicon Valley venture capital firms at their prestigious addresses. Venerable trees framing an ascending road claimed my full attention. Headed west, I imagined a processional of ancients ushering me to a place beyond time.

As I reached the avenue's peak, oaks parted and a bridge lifted me over a discord of cars on Interstate 280. My heart soared like a bird through a liminal shift at the crossroads and carried me to the other side, where I was greeted with a vast and lush panoramic view of the Santa Cruz Mountains. Halfway to my destination, I was now gliding through countryside where stoplights and streetlights were outlawed and open space for wildlife habitat was preserved.

To my left was Stanford University's Jasper Ridge Biological Preserve, 1200 acres of refuge for wild animals and native plants. To my right was the Horse Park at Woodside, 270 acres of wonderland where equestrian activity dotted open pastures and oak-studded hills. Soon Sand Hill Road turned into Portola Road, and I saw a life-giving freshwater marsh before me, home to cattails, herons, ducks, and coots. Then came the wooden sign, "Welcome to Portola Valley."

A few minutes later, I arrived at my destination on the scenic corridor in the heart of this small town, population four thousand. Turning into the driveway, my tires crunching on gravel, I was greeted by a barn, where the historic name Finbarr Ranch was painted on the gable under a set of eight-point deer antlers.

The sun was warm as I walked along a wooden fence thickset with yellow trumpet vines serving nectar to hummingbirds and honeybees. Our ranch manager, Chase, waved hello as he drove by on a tractor. His dog, Riley, wiggled his tail and brushed by my side before bounding off after a squirrel.

As many times as I had done it, I was never quite prepared for the awe I experienced opening the pedestrian gate to an almighty presence of an evergreen-forested mountain. The lap of her base lay before me, holding fourteen acres of orchard colored with organic red apples, green pears, and yellow quinces. I stood there for a few moments, allowing all of my senses to open in devotion to the resplendent beauty that lay on the edge between wilderness and civilization.

Blackbirds were singing, bees were humming, warm air brushed the hairs on my skin, and a potpourri of juicy fruits and wildflowers tickled my nose. In a ceremonial gesture, I took a deep breath and exhaled three times, allowing my abdomen and lungs to fill with clean, fragrant air. I was about to enter my barn — an outward reflection of my heart that had been sub rosa in the making for thirteen years.

From my vantage point as I walked alongside the building, it resembled a farmhouse with off-white horizontal wood lap siding and a metal corrugated roof. But when I turned and presented my back to the orchard, facing the entrance, it reminded me of a Greek temple, New Orleans style. The roof was pitched, and porch columns flanked oversized double doors that were painted a brilliant mosque blue.

Up the three stairs, I slid between a pair of pillars and opened the sapphire-colored portal to another realm. Crossing the threshold, I was stilled by a thick silence. This was a holy place, the house of wild animal spirits who were reborn when I infused their bodies, bones, and parts with my total presence and pure awareness.

Touched by their grace, my body tingled. Art made of bone, claw, horn, tooth, sinew, and fur was exquisitely arranged. As I felt my heart lift from the splendor, it raised my attention to the expansive cathedral ceiling, where bouquets of orange, yellow, and purple dried flowers hung upside down from the rafters. Amidst the heavenly garden, a fully articulated coyote skeleton appeared to be galloping midair near a black-feathered crow who soared with wide wings and a felted gnome on his back.

Drawing my eyes downward to the opposite end of the room, I connected with a longhorn-bull skull at the center of a large built-in altar. In homage to the four elements of earth, fire, air, and water, it was surrounded by two wooden candlesticks laden with wax drippings, a hand-carved quartz crystal chalice embellished with gemstones on a gold stem, and a generous bouquet of wild turkey feathers. Ceremonial relics, from bones to mortars, pestles, and fur, also adorned the shrine.

At the center of the room, twelve high-back barstools surrounded a thick slab of reclaimed teakwood sturdily crafted into a tall rectangular table. Draped over the back of each chair were twelve Polish sheepskins of the finest quality. Each pelt was vegetable tanned, soft and supple, with its own unique shape, texture, and color. Long and straight, short and curly, or medium fluffed pelages varied in tone from brown, to white, golden, or marbled. My hands were drawn to pet them as if they were living, loving, and breathing sheep.

Gazing at the twelve empty chairs around my classroom table, I imagined the women of all ages who would gather here to explore the masks we wear and what's behind them. My heart fluttered to think I would soon be the spiritual feminine elder I had always dreamed of, ready and able to guide women to realize their authentic wildness in a civilized world.

Come with me now on a journey from my childhood to present day. If you are on a path of healing and self-discovery, may my stories of personal truth and transformation show you how to quicken your process.

Chapter Two

nature child

For the strength of the Pack is the Wolf,
and the strength of the Wolf is the Pack.

—*Rudyard Kipling*

Wolf is the holy heartbeat of wilderness. Crying for connection, her hauntingly lonely howl echoes through inner and outer landscapes of thick forest, deep snow, vast grassland, and dry desert. Natural, original, spontaneous, and wild, Wolf drives the pulse of nature. Deeply connected, she lives in a pack that functions and survives as one organism.

Wolf loves, respects, and values her clan. Upon meeting, she and her kin nuzzle each other with noses and whiskers as their tails stir the air and their fur quivers with glee. When puppies are born, doting adults are eager to care for the young ones and raise them at the center of their circle. New life in the pack is celebrated with affectionate touches, whimpers, and whines. Likewise, the death of a clan mate is grieved from the belly with heartbreaking howls and laments.

When I was a child, *The Jungle Book* by Rudyard Kipling was my favorite story. The Kipling tale spoke to me in many ways. I was captivated by the animals who came to life with human characteristics and personalities, and I eagerly absorbed the moral of every story. In my mind I, too, was a nature child raised by a wolf pack—of humans. I resonated strongly with the character Mowgli, and *The Jungle Book* myth became an emblem for my life's journey. It subconsciously taught me the laws of the jungle and how to survive in a civilized world.

Born with the temperament of Wolf, I was birthed late at night under a dark waning balsamic crescent moon, which carried within it the promise of my destiny. Christened Lucinda Bakken Garr, I was imprinted with elements from both my maternal and paternal ancestors.

My parents were twenty when they married and I was born. Two years later, they separated. After that I only saw my father on a few brief occasions. For most of the sixties, in an era when divorce was not common, I lived alone with my mother.

Like a lioness, my mother was strong, fierce, and protective of me. I felt safe in her care. If she had hardships finishing her college degree, establishing a career, and providing for me, I was unaware of them. She did not burden me with her problems and left me to my childhood bliss. Wild, unencumbered by expectations, and free to be myself, I was deeply connected to all aspects of nature. I played in soil, water, and trees. My soul was alive and engaged with a myriad of magical kingdoms—animal, plant, and fairy—into which I delved ever more deeply on the wings of my rich imagination.

My mother lovingly nurtured me with food, shelter, clothing, education, and tribe. As often as she could, Mom planted me at the center of my maternal and paternal birth clans for extended periods of heartfelt emotional sustenance. Nearly every school break—Thanksgiving, Christmas, Easter, and summer—my mom and I drove for eight hours to be with her large family in Oregon. Other times I flew by myself to southern California to stay with my dad's parents, Mimi and Papa Garr.

When Mom and I traveled to Oregon we stayed with her parents, Sweetie and Paps, in their two-story quaint suburban home. Great-grandpa lived there too. His heavy Norwegian accent transported me to an ancient world. I considered the Bakkens my wolf pack, with grandparents, cousins, aunts, and uncles who rallied around me with nuzzles, games, stories, and joy.

My clan anchored me and adored me in my fullness, even when I was feisty, bossy, and bold. When I went to the hospital at three years old to have my tonsils removed, I yelled at the nurse when she gave me a shot, "You dummy!" The elders in my pack retold that story so many times I can still feel their laughs like a song in my belly and their smiles are etched in my mind.

The Bakken lifestyle was small-town and simple, thriving on a currency of heart. I had plenty of pack mates to play with — young cousins and neighborhood children. Filled with imagination, we dressed up in vintage clothing we found at the back of my grandparents' attic. As we roamed the friendly neighborhood on bicycles, we talked and we laughed. In our yards we wrestled and bickered, climbed tree after tree, and ate bushels of wild raspberries and blackberries.

Sweetie and Paps also had a lakefront cabin where I paddled a canoe, caught fish on a line, skied on the water, and pretended to be an amphibian. It was near the lake's shore where I swam and connected with frogs — eye to eye — on the threshold between air and water. Mesmerized by their stillness, I magnified my senses to become one with their kind. The smell of dark soil enriched from decay filled my lungs as I gently touched jellied, round eggs dotted black at each center. Soft-eyed and heartfelt, communicating but wordless, we dipped below the surface and glided in harmony like mermaids through a forest of lily pads.

Mimi and Papa also had a profound influence on my life. They owned and lived on Garr Ranch, a 350-acre Eden of vast and diverse wilderness, cattle farming, and orchards. Young, carefree, and wide open, I wholeheartedly immersed myself and reveled in the nature of that place. It was a life-force that vigorously pumped ruby-red blood through my veins.

I do not remember much about my father, but I do know that my grandfather loved me dearly and told me so. Some nights before bed we went onto the screened porch, and I sat on his lap in a rocker. When my ear touched his chest, he wrapped his strong arms around me. The warm evening air was heavy as it hummed a night song of crickets. My grandfather's voice was soothing. It rolled with a rhythm that matched the back-and-forth motion of our chair. I can still smell the sweetness of scotch and water on his breath and hear the tinkle of melting ice in his glass.

Mimi was the grand matriarch at the helm of my experience at Garr Ranch. With my beloved Papa by her side, she set the stage for magic to unfold by offering her grandchildren nature, freedom, and fun. Every day was an adventure for my four cousins and me. We rode in open-air jeeps on hot, dusty roads, picnicked near the river, rolled the bare arms and legs of our bodies in tall grasses, and steered with our feet as we raced down steep hills on a "Flexy Flyer," a wooden sled on wheels. Other days we climbed up into haylofts, watched cowboys rope and brand cattle, harvested almonds in the orchard, fiercely competed at tether ball, and screamed as we flew on the zip line. When Mimi gave us freedom to explore on our own, I often found myself swirling in the currents of a stream, sliding my body over mossy-smooth rocks and dipping my head under low-hanging sun-dappled leaves.

Easter day at Garr Ranch was a flowering festival for the senses. Morning time was gentle as we cuddled soft baby bunnies, lambs, and chicks. Midday, things heated up as we yipped, yelled, and darted along the river, searching for rainbow-colored eggs to put in our baskets. Being on the alert for rattlesnakes hidden under rocks or slithering through the grass heightened the thrill of our hunt. In the afternoon, it was time for a donkey piñata stuffed with fantastic candies and prizes. Our imaginations were filled with delight at the thought of spectacular toys, miniature games, and confections. Electricity ran through our bodies as we watched our grandpa use thick, coarse rope to tie the beast to a tree limb. We took turns covering our eyes with a bandana and using a full-sized wooden bat to play the game. Our swings were fierce. One by one, my cousins and I were desperate to bust the piñata wide open so we could fall to the ground and claw for our loot. I spent hours inspecting, admiring, and savoring my treasures with pure joy and true love.

We groaned when Mimi made us take naps, but I secretly loved it. My favorite spot was an old outbuilding separate from the main house. It was small with a loft that barely fit two twin beds. Open windows with screens invited hot, dry air to seep in and blanket my skin. The smell of earth and old wood was heavy, filling my nose and lungs with comfort and peace as I slid into slumber.

Just before dusk, Mimi would grab her chicken-shaped glass candy dish. It was time for our nightly ritual. We climbed an awesome giant boulder that looked so big it could have been a mountain. At the top, we lay on our backs scanning the sky, each of us hoping to be number one.

Number one squealed and pointed when he or she saw the first star to appear in the night sky. Number one got to lift the chicken's lid and take one tiny hard candy for a prize. Luckily, it was the same reward for numbers two, three, four, and five. We played until the sky was so full of starlight that the yellow glass chicken was empty.

Then, when I was eleven my mother remarried, and my life changed dramatically. Although her new husband adopted me and welcomed me into his family, my nurturing connections to the Bakken and Garr clans were left behind. I never visited Garr Ranch again, and it was decades before I returned to Oregon. Suddenly I was in new territory without the comfort and security of my familiar wolf packs.

Today blended families are more common, and there are books, support groups, and conversations to assist with the process of forming them. This was not so when I was a child. Raised in an era when people suppressed their sadness, anger, and grief, my parents did not know what to do with the emotions I expressed. They wanted me to be happy and grateful for all I had gained, and they could not imagine why I would ever be sad.

When I howled, moped, or grieved like a wolf, my behavior was viewed as disruptive and unfair to those around me. Drawing on Kipling's laws of the jungle, I soon learned to keep peace with my lords by obeying their rules. But there were consequences to be paid when my spontaneous thoughts, feelings, and emotions were denied.

That is when my original nature started to erode.

Chapter Three

a wolf among lions

To be ourselves causes us to be exiled by many others,
and yet to comply with what others want causes us
to be exiled from ourselves.

—*Clarissa Pinkola Estés*

Grounded in the rich, fragrant soil of my original birth clans, I had once been a vibrant blooming tree. When a tornado of change ripped out my roots at age eleven, I was tossed, turned, and swirled in a funnel cloud that sucked at my soul's essence and slammed my body down on the ground. Dazed and confused, I felt detached from parts of myself. My thoughts went from solid to blurry. Disoriented, in a foreign territory amidst a new kind of people, I felt like a wolf among lions.

Wolves thrive in a cooperative family lifestyle, reminiscent of ancient indigenous tribes. A typical pack includes a mother, father, offspring, and helpers who all collectively care for, play with, and rear the puppies. Alpha pack leaders are confident. They manage with swift decisiveness, leveraging the strengths of each clan mate. With deep bonds and essential trust, a wolf pack hunts, plays, eats, sleeps, and breathes as one organism.

Lions on the other hand typically live in a pride comprised of two subgroups: a coalition of males and a crèche of lionesses with cubs.

A male lion's role is to sire offspring and protect the pride, while females primarily hunt and raise the children collectively. Within the pride, adult males and females come together to feed or mate. At other times, they mostly consort with their own kind. Although the new family I found myself in was not exactly a pride, it certainly resembled one in some ways, but with only one male — and he was king of the jungle.

My mother's courtship with my soon-to-be father was fast. Within one year they met, married, moved to a new town, and birthed a baby. In a flash, I was uprooted, and my connections to school, friends, home, town, birth clans, and Garr Ranch were severed. In many ways, I lost my mom too. She had her own process of transition to endure and new family members to care for.

Soon after the move, in seventh grade, I hit puberty, and my body started to bleed without warning. For my generation, sexual education at school was minimal, and it was not common for mothers to talk with their daughters about body changes, periods, and sex. Becoming a young woman caught me off guard, and the hush around it hinted at shame.

My mom sent me to the bathroom with a box of tampons. That was it. I sat on the toilet feeling inadequate as I tried shoving cardboard tubes into parts of my body I didn't understand. Despite several tries, I could not get it right. I did my best, but the poorly inserted tampon hung low and chafed me throughout the school day. Every step caused me pain and humiliation. I wondered why was this happening.

For years Mom's belly was swollen and her arms were filled with one, two, and then three babies. While she was busy caring for her new cubs, Dad was my guiding force. A good man, my new father legally adopted me and parented me as if I were his own flesh and blood. I was blessed when he gifted me with a traditional nuclear family, tangible wealth, elite opportunities, and prestige.

Although my assets looked great on paper, the assimilation was rough. Turned 180 degrees away from the ways of my previous clan and lifestyle, I struggled to learn and adapt to the rules of my new father's kingdom. Sometimes he explicitly told me what to do, how to look, and how to behave. Other times I was left alone, learning how to survive through keen observation and trial and error. And that is how it went for the next fifteen years as I was predominantly influenced by a masculine view of womanhood.

One of the first things my dad did was give me a horse. "Every girl should have one," he said. It had never been my desire to own or care for a horse. In fact, I was intimidated by their size. I know now he was well intentioned. He built a stall on our property and set me up with a horse who had been put out to pasture. I'm sure he thought we were both lonely and needed each other.

Dan was a scruffy chestnut-colored thoroughbred (I think) with a white star on his forehead. My dad gave me a few perfunctory instructions, but for the most part I was left to my own devices. I recalled riding on Mimi's horse with her at Garr Ranch, but I had never ridden alone. I was scared of Dan, and he knew it.

Our new home was set on the side of a hill in Portola Valley, California, with stunning views of a forested canyon, faraway lights, and a distant blue ocean bay. The driveway to our property was formidable, short, and steep. To get Dan from his stall up to the roadside trails was a feat in and of itself. There was no room to walk or warm up at the bottom, so we just had to go for it. The hill's slope to the street felt near perpendicular. Pinpricks of terror ripped through my body as I spurred Dan to lunge up the vertical trail. With every thrust forward, I bounced and slid back, holding on for my life.

Reaching the top, Dan was always short-winded, agitated, and spooked from the run. He often stopped and refused to go forward on the trail. When he did that, I felt panic in the pit of my stomach, for I knew what was coming next. He'd flip his nose up, lay his ears flat, crack his tail like a whip, rear his body, buck several times, then take off like a bat out of hell down the remote trail that lay before us.

I dreaded my time with Dan. I was terrified to ride and care for him, but I did not feel free to be honest with my father about his gift. Speaking my truth when it did not align with my parents' values was considered an ungrateful response to all the abundance they bestowed on me. When I failed to ride my horse or clean up the poop in his stall, my father joked that I was lazy and irresponsible. Although his words were supposedly delivered in jest, they hurt.

My experience with Dan taught me rule number one in our pride: pretend to be happy and grateful for everything, even if you feel otherwise.

When I wasn't in school or riding my horse, I often hung out alone in my bedroom. Perhaps it was due to the changing hormones of puberty. Or maybe that room was my only safe space and a sanctuary I needed because of my introverted nature. It didn't matter.

One night my dad's parents came to visit, and I didn't come out of my cave. My dad was furious. He thought I was rude and really let me have it in a way that I had not experienced before. It scared me. The focus in his eyes and the swell of his growl left me frozen as he asserted, "When someone comes to our house, you get off your ass and walk out of your room. Look people in the eye and make conversation." It was clear that, unwittingly, I had embarrassed my dad with my behavior, and his anger let me know it was personal.

That day I learned rule number two: go out of your way to charm people no matter how you feel on the inside.

Soon I discovered that dazzling my dad's family and friends was easier than riding my horse. I learned how to shapeshift into a darling who could win over a room full of adults. Gushing with positive energy, I reached out to grown-ups one at a time. I engaged them with questions and coaxed out stories, but most of all I attentively listened. And then I moved on, making the rounds to uplift more people with my full presence.

When my dad received compliments about me, he swelled with pride and let me know it. What began as a performance to please other people and avoid my father's ire turned into a curiosity of sorts. I learned a lot about grown-ups by hearing them talk and observing their behaviors. I was especially drawn to introverts, underdogs, and elders. I suppose they were mirrors for me. This was when I had my first premonition that I would someday be a wise elder with high purpose.

Although my role as the darling served our pride's image and pleased my parents, the one area where I continued to fail and embarrass them was my physical appearance. With the loss of my birth clans there remained a sadness that I felt as an ache in my belly and chest. I felt empty and alone. Eating more food than my body needed was my futile attempt to fill that void with something. Of course food was no replacement for authentic soulful connections and only served to fill out the human flesh of my body beyond the cultural norm.

For most of my teens and twenties, my weight was fifteen to thirty pounds above the mainstream ideal. It was a challenge to find outfits that flattered my frame in a way that pleased my parents. They always asked me ahead of time what I would be wearing to a gathering or an event, as if I might blow it. Preparing for any public appearance, even the grocery store, filled me with anxiety, especially if my hair was frizzy or my face had a pimple or my skin was pale from winter.

I learned from my dad that tanned skin was desirable. He even coached me as I sunbathed, telling me when to turn over so my coloring would be even, front to back. Before I went out the door to a party, he took his finger and twirled it, which meant I was to turn around so he could inspect my appearance from all angles. On the occasions that I lost weight, looked pretty, or dazzled the crowd, my dad would purr loudly and share his approval through verbal praise, hugs, and gifts. But when I was lazy, unruly, or shy, it provoked him to snarl his displeasure, and I felt my heart tremble.

The summer before my senior year in high school, my family rented a house on the beach with another family who had four kids close to my age. Each of us brought more than one friend. There were a slew of teenagers with us that week; most of them were super good-looking.

When we returned from vacation, my parents sat me down for a talk. Dad told me Mom and he were embarrassed about how I looked in a bikini. He suggested I go on a diet and offered to enroll me in a urine-injection program because supposedly there is a hormone in certain types of urine that promotes rapid weight loss of one pound per day.

On the program my daily food intake was severely restricted to five hundred calories of selected protein and vegetables, with no fat or carbs allowed. Every Monday through Friday after school, I was required to drive myself to a doctor's office where I was weighed in, documented, tracked, and injected with pee. At home when I walked through the door — first thing — my dad asked for the number. On the weekends when the office was closed, it was my dad's job to stab me with syringes full of urine.

One afternoon as I drove to the weigh-in, I was overcome with distress. With no one to talk to, alone with my feelings, I wondered how to reconcile the hunger that was gnawing at my gut against the consequences of allaying it. Each time I cheated, the doctor, the nurse, and my dad knew it, because the scales never lied. When my number went up, my face immediately flushed and I felt shame burning under my skin. I was helpless, trapped in a riddle I could not unlock: to starve was to live, and to eat was to die. As deprivation sucked at my heart and my will, I began to move in and out of consciousness. I felt like I was floating outside my body, inside the car. When a blur of vehicles passed me by, I saw bright-red lights and flashes of yellow, but I had no awareness of anything tangible.

Suddenly the volume on my radio turned up, and I heard Steven Tyler howling the "Dream On" crescendo. It felt like the call of a wolf. The vibration of his cry made my soul shiver and rattled my pulse to bring me back into my body. After the appointment, I drove to 7-Eleven and purchased three king-sized Snickers bars. I swallowed them swiftly, one after another, as if I were gulping a glass of ice water under the hot desert sun.

The urine-injection program was not my first or last diet, because of rule number three in our pride: be thin and beautiful according to mainstream standards, even if it kills you.

I worked hard for fifteen years to abide by the three golden rules of our kingdom, feeling it was my duty to master the external presentation of myself in order to be of value and make my parents proud. Their lessons were important to help me integrate with society, but the other half of myself was not talked about or even acknowledged. Overemphasizing my human nature clipped my soul and knocked me off balance.

Fragmented and shaped by forces outside of me, I was no longer a healthy wild wolf. When a part of me fell off the spectrum of wild to become a good girl tamed by the expectations of others, I lost touch with the honesty and fullness of my original nature. To further the damage, a part of me desperately clung to the shadow end of wild's spectrum. This imbalance played out through addictions that numbed or distracted me from the pain I experienced hiding my truth and full self.

Inflicted with a rabid kind of wildness, an inner savage beast was unleashed, capable of horrific self-destruction. Lacking a connection to the navigation system of my intuition, instincts, and feelings, I followed the crowd and misdirected my pent-up wild energy. Voraciously devouring anything that might ease my famine, I consumed food, cocaine, speed, and quaaludes and had several one-night stands.

University was not on my radar as a young teen. I did not have a clue what happened there or why I should go. But at some point, my dad said, "You're going to college." So I applied to three schools that had good weather. The University of Arizona was my number-one pick by a long shot because it would ensure my best tan and good hair. San Diego State and UCLA were second choices due to the seasonal beach fog that would frizz my straightened mane. All three schools accepted me. I pleaded for Arizona. Dad chose the school with the best reputation. He said, "You're going to UCLA."

Lions and wolves are top predators who live in social communities, but a very important distinction between the two species came to my awareness later in life. Lions are a bit more independent and self-centered than wolves. Lion has a royal demeanor and likes to be served, while Wolf's nature is to serve the pack. Lions are rulers and wolves are leaders. In general, rulers impose domination and control over bodies and resources while leaders earn respect and guide those who are willing.

My dad — influenced by his upbringing and the values of his era — taught me how to look, think, and act. And I bought it hook, line, and sinker. Ready or not, at age eighteen, I left my family to become a full-blown yuppie in pursuit of the materialistic American dream. I knew the promise. It echoed throughout the media and surrounding culture: If you are pretty, thin, rich, and accomplished — with tangible evidence to prove it — you will be happy and loved. I was certainly aching for that, but Los Angeles was a tough spot for me to land, because it magnified all the demons I had struggled with since age eleven. I was truly a wolf among lions.

Chapter Four

disconnected from nature

We're so engaged in doing things to achieve purposes
of outer value that we forget the inner value.

—*Joseph Campbell*

Wolves are keen observers, deeply connected to all that surrounds them. They intimately know the weather, water, terrain, and their environment by engaging with all of their senses. Cohesive in a pack, they thrive in a state of full presence and are acutely aware of all creatures in their territory.

Caribou, buffalo, moose, and elk are bigger than wolves, and yet they are a pack's primary food source. It only takes one swift kick of an ungulate's hoof to crack a wolf's jaw or skull, or one stab of an antler or horn to pierce a wolf's flesh like a knife. When a pack of wolves hunts for sustenance, their lives depend on awareness, cooperation, intellect, and endurance.

To begin the hunt, an agile wolf may deliberately cause chaos by running straight into a herd while others fan out to surround and contain the prey within a moving barrier. Amidst the turmoil, a strong wolf will look for opportunity and try to take down a young, old, or sick target as another wolf moves in for support. All the while—in a focused pursuit that could last for miles—the pack remains fluid and works as one unit, making high-speed adjustments in response to the shifting landscape and behavior of the prey. Through attunement, collaboration, push, pull, and flow, each pack member knows exactly what to do at all times. It's the invisible threads of deep awareness and connection that weave a wolf pack together in unison.

By the time I was seventeen, I was completely disconnected from nature—both inside and outside of me. Although I enjoyed being outdoors, I was not a wild wolf tuned into the environment and fully engaged with all of my senses. No longer communing with animals, flowers, and trees, I was not even aware of their presence. All of my focus and energy was directed into following a formula that was drilled into me by my father.

His bottom line was this: Be happy all the time. Be strong. Sad days and a full range of feelings are abnormal, disruptive, and not fair to those around you. Never talk back to your elders. Only say things that are pleasant and engaging. Be the most beautiful woman in the room wherever you go. Work hard. Marry a rich man who is tall with long legs. Make the family proud.

I believed my father, and I knew I was fortunate that he paid all of my bills. Armed with his money in my pocket and his voice in my head, I left for college sincerely wanting to please him. I soon discovered that would not be so easy to do. The greater Los Angeles area is a land of beautiful people, many of them aspiring actors or models. In a sea of flawlessly gorgeous young women, at every turn I saw luscious, styled hair; sexy, smart clothing; sparkling-white teeth; plump pink lips; and smooth, sun-kissed bodies. More than once I heard a random guy brag there was no point in having a girlfriend with so much booty at hand.

It was hard for me to compete. The skills I had developed for charming elders did not naturally work with my peers. Perhaps I was just insecure and overly self-conscious, believing that people, in general, placed a high value on physical beauty. Oh sure, there were some days after a crash starvation diet when my tan body could fit into a sexy outfit and the arid weather worked in my favor. With no frizz on my long blonde hair and a statuesque frame to complement my outfit, I felt like a knockout, and my personality matched how I felt. But most of the time, I felt unlovable for being overly curvy in clothes that were not hip or flattering and for having big hair that was unruly in humid weather. Most of the time I tried and failed to measure up to the mark of good looks in Los Angeles, and I honestly believed it was embarrassing for my peers to be seen with me on my unattractive days.

In my teens and twenties, I aimed for and labored to be part of the popular crowds. I sought their acceptance as a stamp of approval to confirm I was OK. As a freshman at UCLA, I went through sorority rush but failed to receive a bid. That was a major blow that left me feeling rejected by female peers. Sophomore year I was urged by a friend to try once more. With renewed hope, I rushed a second time, and again I was not chosen.

Recklessly ignoring the clues, on a Saturday night, I auditioned for a Little Sister program at one of the top fraternities. My heart pounded as I stood there in a long lineup with girls waiting to dance a number. Alcohol was supplied and encouraged, so I shot two kamikazes just before it was my turn to step onto the makeshift stage. At first the bright lights were blinding, but soon I saw the red shine of bloodshot predator eyes leering at me. The sweltering room was full of drunken hyenas with sneering lips and long pointed canines. That night I sacrificed my soul and performed to please with the hope for external approval, but once again I was not chosen.

One of my good friends from high school also attended UCLA. Her next-door neighbor from home told us his fraternity brothers thought we were cool, but if we wanted a date we had to lose weight. Then we heard a story about a guy who wrote an anonymous letter to his own girlfriend suggesting she shed some pounds.

Soon after that, my dad offered to give me a Porsche if I lost twenty pounds. So I did. That car was my sweetest revenge. In Los Angeles everyone knows "you are what you drive." My apartment was located behind Fraternity Row. Every day going to and fro I would inevitably end up at a red light, facing two fraternities in my bright-yellow Porsche 911. I felt powerful watching guys drool from afar as I revved up my engine and raced past their ogling eyes with long blonde hair flying out of my window.

The car boosted my confidence and helped me find a groove. After that I stayed in Los Angeles through the summers and only went home to visit my family at Thanksgiving and Christmas. In one of my classes I met a strikingly handsome, super adorable, nonfraternity guy. His name was Ayden. Although I could not describe our chemistry with words, I knew it was comfortable and life-giving. Looking back, it's clear he loved me for all the right reasons and valued who I was on the inside. At that point in time, he knew me better than I did. Stuck in my superficial ways, I continued to emphasize fast cars, beauty, and fame. Ayden did not like my royal side, and he teased me about it. He also did not like it when I drank alcohol.

The upside was that I had a boyfriend, and we were madly in love. Ayden was a surfer, tall with long legs, smart, and *fun*. We laughed and we laughed and we laughed. He loved my full figure and thought I was crazy to be trapped by diets. He took me to old-fashioned drive-in movie theatres in his Volkswagen camper van, and we gorged on juicy gourmet hamburgers dripping with mayonnaise, pickles, and catsup with a side of hand-cut french fries and thick vanilla milkshakes. He thought I was beautiful and told me so often.

On school breaks, we went on adventures, exploring the coast and camping in his van. I loved to run my fingers through his thick, long, wild hair, and his hands were attracted to the curves on my body like superconductor magnets. He bought us a pair of matching beach cruisers (stylish upright bicycles with fat tires) that we rode throughout Westwood and all over campus. We did our schoolwork together in the library stacks. I helped him pass art history, and he helped me pass astronomy.

Ayden and I studied hard, had deep talks, and played all the time. I felt the strings of our love and genuine connection pulling my soul back down into my body. Sure that my parents would be proud of me for attracting a good-looking, intelligent, and capable young man (with long legs), we jumped into my car and headed north. I was excited for my parents to meet him.

I don't recall how long we stayed or what the interactions were like; all I remember is the ambush at the end of our visit. When Ayden went out to the car just before we were leaving, my dad pulled me aside. With his most intense look, he narrowed his eyes and lowered his voice to deliver a message. With a slow and deliberate precision, he said, "If you *ever* bring that arrogant punk into my home again, I will cut you off. How dare you!"

Stunned, I stood there in silence as he growled, "I know it took you two days to drive up here from LA so you must have stayed in a motel. *I* gave you that car and *I* pay all of your expenses. I do *not* give you money to finance a guy so he can take you to bed!"

Injured and breathless, I somehow turned and made my way out to the car. The trip back to Los Angeles was quiet and uncomfortable. I was confused and ashamed of choosing the wrong guy. Once we were back in LA, I broke up with Ayden. Even though my feelings for him did not line up with my father's assessment, I felt like a bad little girl and allowed my dad's authority to overrule my own. Feeling sick to my stomach for getting the rules of love wrong, I worried about how disappointing I must be to everyone else that I knew.

Soon after I graduated from UCLA, I went back to school and earned a master's degree in business administration from Pepperdine. By age twenty-four, my life looked pretty good in pictures and on paper, but deep down inside I was lonely and longing for something I could not explain. Ravenous in my desire to prove I was lovable and determined to be free of my dad's financial control over me, my pain turned into anger and fueled a fire inside my belly.

Drawing on my predatory nature, I became fierce and focused as I zeroed in on the hunt for a prestigious job with high pay. It was 1984, and IBM met all of my criteria. As a large, established blue-chip-stock company, IBM had name recognition and power in a high-growth industry with plenty of career-path options. Big Blue was the ultimate fraternity and stamp of approval. I wanted in.

I knew the interview process at IBM was highly competitive, lengthy, and grueling. So I went to work, studying the art of interviewing, IBM's corporate culture, and their product line. This was before cell phones, laptops, and the Internet, so I tracked down information in collegiate and public libraries. Digging deep, I read journals I found in the stacks, and I spent hours on microfiche readers. I also read books about IBM, studied their competitors, and memorized a bevy of annual reports.

What I enjoyed most was reading John T. Molloy's book *Dress for Success*, which revealed all of the secrets I craved for "power dressing." The first thing I did was cut off my long, wild hair and tame it into a bob. Next, I invested in four calculated uniforms guaranteed to help me project the right image. My matching fitted blazers and skirts were made of fine gabardine wool. My suit palette was navy blue to dark gray, pinstripe or plain, and set off with a crisp, white long-sleeve, button-down shirt. To accent the look, I wore a colorful hand-knotted silk tie and carried a monogrammed leather briefcase.

To practice my well-studied technique, I set up dozens of interviews with random high-tech companies. At each meeting I learned something new and gained more and more confidence. These exercises helped me anticipate and prepare for a broad range of questions, personalities, and systems. In no time, I was an expert at the interview game, and I received boatloads of offers I never considered. They were hares in a field when my eye was on elk.

During the interview process at IBM I beat out thousands of other candidates and was ultimately chosen. It felt great at first, but working there was a new challenge. Most of the trainees had technical degrees in computer science or engineering. Not me. I didn't know a thing about technology.

I did my job and got good reviews, but my mind was not scientific, and the IBM product line bored me. I could not imagine spending the rest of my life selling giant computers and storage devices to high-tech executives who lived in the stark gray bowels of a corporate data-processing center. Without a pack to guide and support my pursuit of sustenance, I had preyed on a job that risked the life of my soul. I may have looked slick and shiny on the outside, but my insides were knotted and churning.

By my twenty-seventh birthday, I realized something was wrong. I was living "the dream" with three girls in a condo near the beach in Santa Monica, and I commuted to IBM in my Porsche. I was suntanned, blonde, and pretty, not to mention social, kind, and smart too. My credentials looked great on paper. I was responsible. I paid my bills on time, and I earned a proper living. I had done everything my father and the surrounding culture told me to do. The promise was that if I did as they said, I'd be happy, loved, and adored. Therefore, it made no sense that I was miserable. And then one day, I finally felt the big lie in my body.

Sitting in a customer meeting, I felt assaulted. The smell of old coffee made me nauseous. The monotonous whir of giant mainframe computers grated on my nerves while supercold air conditioning chilled me to the bone and spoiled the air that I breathed. I felt barren and disheartened when it suddenly hit me. I had been tricked by the media, my family, and the dominant social order.

Distraught, I flew home to have a talk with my dad in person. I told him I wanted to leave IBM. As he encouraged me to stick with it for professional reasons, my eyes welled up with tears. To his credit, he saw my pain and immediately said, "Come home. You can live with us."

In those days, IBM employees were lifers. It was rare and shocking if someone left the family. I did it anyway. As soon as my things were packed up, I drove north to live in my parents' basement. Leaving behind my past and arriving home with no identity, purpose, goals, or friends, I also arrived with no reason to live.

I spiraled into a deep depression. Staring at one wall, I lay there for weeks, releasing a range of soft cries and loud sobs. Eventually, as the weeks turned into months, I ran out of tears. Still every task felt insurmountable. I could not make my body get up to exercise, take a shower, or even sit outside under a tree.

No one I knew could relate to my despair, not my friends nor my parents. Whenever I tried to talk about intimate, honest feelings—before, during, and after Los Angeles—the responses were something like this: "You are so lucky. I don't feel sorry for you! You have everything. You are tall, blonde, and pretty. You have money and a good job. You have a family. Your parents are still married, and they are affluent to boot. Get over it and stop feeling sorry for yourself."

I knew it was true. I was lucky and blessed. But that made me feel worse. I found myself wondering how I could possibly be sad. *There must be something wrong with me*, I thought.

As dark thoughts looped in my mind with no resolution, I wondered if I was crazy. It felt as if I were standing tightly pressed between two cement walls that were smashing my nose, chest, and toes. Trapped, I only saw two ways out: slide to the right and return to high-tech as a yuppie or slide to the left and commit suicide to release myself from this hell.

Going to the left felt better than the right. For hours and days, I fantasized about various ways to end my life. Imagining my blood and the pain made me faint, so there was no way I could slit my wrists. Instead of a garage we had a carport, so I could not poison myself with carbon monoxide. I did not know how to make a noose. And of course my parents were health nuts, so there were no pills to be found in the house.

My mother vacillated. Sometimes she quietly sat by my side with genuine compassion. Other times she gave me a pep talk with a "get up and go" attitude. My sisters were busy teenagers at thirteen, fourteen, and fifteen years old. I hardly ever saw them. My father was quite annoyed. When he came down to visit, it irked him to find me on the couch, limp and ragged with a drooping face and messy hair. One time he sat at my feet and made an effort to be nice, but I was unresponsive. It caused him to launch into a lecture. As he tried to coax me right out of the house, his words fell on deaf ears and slid off my listless body.

Finally, one day my apathy (which presented to him as me being lazy) triggered a rumble and growl. "I've had enough of this! Your mother and I have let you sit here and rest long enough. You are disrupting the family, and it's not fair to your little sisters."

The truth in his words scared me enough to perk up. I didn't want to be a burden; I just didn't know what to do. My defenses had collapsed, and my mind drifted off thinking of all the things he had said to me over the years that I was never able to question. When he finished his speech, I lifted my head from the pillow to face him and said, "Dad, when you say 'all women are a pain in the ass' out in public, and you admonish young men to never get married, it hurts me. I am a woman."

He responded quickly, with sass, "Well, that's how I feel."

I looked at him and cried, "I want to die! I want to kill myself!"

And he said, "Well, hurry up and do it, if that's what you want."

Devastated and confused, I had no comeback and fell silent.

I was a caged and defeated animal lying on the couch and staring at the wall. As I contemplated my life and myself, I felt trapped. Cut off from my intuition, instinct, and spontaneity, I was ruled by the voices in my head. What I didn't know was that the voices were not mine. They were the result of outside conditioning, which I had never learned — or been encouraged — to question. Worse, I didn't realize that the source of my thoughts and beliefs actually mattered, because they were creating my reality.

My healing could only begin with a passionate quest to remember my inner value.

Chapter Five

lone wolf

If you don't know where you are going,
any road will get you there.

—*George Harrison*

Within a wolf pack there is usually one male alpha and one female alpha who lead and who mate with each other. Other wolves, often referred to as betas or omegas, are assigned various jobs that contribute to the whole clan, from hunting to guarding to nannying. If a nonbreeding wolf is determined to mate, he or she must somehow become a top leader to earn that privilege or resolve to exit the pack.

Breaking off from the pack is risky. Most wolves die when they set out on their own, but some lone wolves are tough, possessing the grit of an alpha. They are driven by a strong instinct to align with their intrinsic nature. If a lone wolf with alpha characteristics is able to survive separation and ultimately finds a mate, the pair will make puppies and lead their own pack.

In the midst of my suicidal depression, it was my mom who gave me another option. She begged me to seek professional help. Reluctant, heavy, and dragging, I agreed to attend an appointment she scheduled for me. I know it was hard for her to suggest a psychologist because her greatest fear was that my problems were her fault, and she was sure that therapy was all about blaming the parents.

Dr. Thomas was a godsend. I was twenty-seven years old, and he was the first person who listened to my full story with compassion. Talking about myself freely for one hour was a novelty. Being deeply heard was revolutionary. Knowing I was not being judged and that he would not use my stories for gossip opened me up and created trust. Getting in touch with my own voice and learning about human psychology was epic.

In the safe place of Dr. Thomas's office, I slowly began to heal from the inside out. As I talked, my long-buried thoughts, words, and emotions at last burst into the atmosphere. It was cleansing to release what I had been holding inside. Therapy created a space for my real self to seep in, for me to take charge and be my own witness. I became more objective, listening to my words as they moved outside of my head.

Prior to working with a psychologist, I had no clear understanding of feelings and emotions. Our family motto was be happy, thin, rich, and strong. As a byproduct of the era my parents grew up in, histrionics were feared as indicative of mental illness. Being sad or grumpy was not allowed. Even the slightest bad mood was a burden to my mom and dad, disrupting their control of perfection.

Dr. Thomas encouraged me to move out of my parents' house ASAP. Since my father's mother had recently transitioned to a nursing home, my dad said I could live in her condominium. I was grateful that he helped me in that way. The separation gave me space to breathe and gain clarity. Soon after that, I found a job. I went back to high-tech because it was the only thing that I knew. Plus, it paid well, and I needed the money.

Orgdata Inc. was a rapidly growing publicly held global software company in Silicon Valley. I was hired in the marketing communications department, even though I had no writing experience. Luckily my new boss took me under her wing and taught me how to write brochures. The initial process was agonizing for both of us, but my extensive training at IBM combined with her patience and guidance launched my career. In a short period of time, I received several managerial promotions with significant pay raises and a windowed office.

For nearly five years, my life was consumed with therapy and career. I worked twelve hours a day, mostly socialized with coworkers, went on a few dates, and had a brief love affair. My weekly commitment to Dr. Thomas was serious. He was esteemed, expensive, and time consuming. I consistently carved out two hours from my work week to travel and meet with him, and I was diligent about working on myself in between our sessions.

Dr. Thomas helped me analyze a myriad of human beliefs and behaviors in the context of how they were healthy or destructive to me. I took his insights and then applied them to my daily life by observing and mentally tracking my thoughts, behaviors, emotions, words, and actions. In sessions we analyzed my goals, progress, and setbacks. It was interesting and required an ongoing honesty, awareness, and presence with myself.

My therapy was a big family secret that was never acknowledged or discussed amongst us. My parents never asked me what I talked about with Dr. Thomas or if they could help. I organized a family meeting once, just my mom, my dad, and me. I wanted to speak my truth and share my feelings. Most likely I was not tactful in my approach, because my mom stood up and walked out after five minutes. For a long time after that, her silence was thick.

Determined to understand the true meaning of life and happiness, I decided to pull back from my parents and distance myself from their influence and the triggers that set off my emotional responses. I wanted to change and become self-defined. Although our houses were only twenty minutes apart, for the next five years, until I was married, I rarely saw my family — usually just for Thanksgiving, Christmas, and Easter.

Going home on holidays triggered my insecurities and created a lot of anxiety. I was uncomfortable with myself and worried about my physical, verbal, and emotional presentation. There was a sea of beauty in my family that rivaled that of Los Angeles. My mother was a dead ringer for Linda Evans, a star on the hit television series *Dynasty*. The Castillo girls, my sisters, were legendary for their knockout looks. All three were blessed, head to toe, with classic features, including awesome long, thick hair that was never frizzy. My sisters were everything I tried to be and could not. They looked great in hip fashion, they had fun and engaging personalities, they were super popular, and they fit into the mainstream culture effortlessly. My parents were proud of them. Even though they were twelve to fifteen years younger than I was, I envied my sisters and compared myself to them.

My mother is an incredible artist and homemaker. She is clever and prolific, rivaling Martha Stewart. She can design, construct, create, cook, sew, draw, or grow just about anything she desires. From a young age, I knew it would be impossible for me to follow in her footsteps. Observing her and other female role models as they cooked, served, cleaned, and crafted left me uninspired. My mom did not go out of her way to apprentice me either. It was her passion to feed, nurture, and delight the family while we gathered, relaxed, and bonded. When I did try to help, it was frustrating for both of us because I could not match her perfection.

On winter holidays, when I opened the door to my mother's realm, my senses were greeted with the magic of her signature feminine ways. The scent of a golden roasting turkey—or some other fabulous meal—escorted me across the threshold to a hearth fire's glow. The decor was always festive, with themes of the season sprinkled throughout every room. At Christmas she created a wonderland with dolls, lights, trains, trees, and stuffed animals. Presents were hand-wrapped in colorful fabrics and tied with cloth ribbons to express her original, homespun style. On every occasion her table was uniquely dressed with color, character, and warmth. Her universe wowed every person who was invited in.

Whether it was a holiday or just an ordinary dinner, it was tradition to gather around Mom while she prepared a feast in the kitchen. We talked, drank, and nibbled with light hearts while she seriously labored before us. Our eyes and mouths watered as we watched her masterfully whip up a vibrant and nourishing array of dishes, all made from scratch with the finest and freshest ingredients.

When it was time for dinner, Mom was always the last to join us because there was more to do in the kitchen. Despite our pleas for her to sit down, she encouraged us to start without her and "eat while it's hot." Eventually she would drift to the table with a tired face and distant eyes. It was clear she had poured all of herself—and more—into the festivities and had nothing left to give, not even a smile.

Mom never fully relaxed at the dinner table, always considering more work to be done. After quietly swallowing two or three bites, she would hurry back to the kitchen and begin preparing dessert or cleaning up while we continued with the family merriment. Watching her in the kitchen, I felt guilty enjoying the pleasures of her sacrifice. I wanted to help her, but I didn't know how to do it her way. I felt like her talent and standards were way out of my league.

For me, all of the magic unraveled the second I saw her leave the dining room table. I wish I'd known how to say "Please sit down and just be with us. I don't care about the decorations or the meal without you." Part of me felt sad and cheated that I lost my mom to housewifery. Another part felt inadequate by comparison, which made me scared to become a housewife. Add in that I felt awkward about my hair, figure, and clothes compared to the rest of the family, and it was often hard for me to contain my emotions.

Complicating the situation, my mother confessed that she was scared of my reactions and moods. She told me she "walked on eggshells" when I was near. And no wonder! I was a fragile work in progress. When I felt insecure, emotional, or defensive I could deliver a sharp cut with one comment to my mom or one of my sisters. Those evenings frequently ended with at least one of us in tears, and I was blamed for ruining the holiday.

Breaking off from my family was a risk, and I took it. At age twenty-nine, I pulled away from the security of my family's power to individuate and become my true self. To symbolize my independence, I financed a new Nissan and returned the yellow Porsche to my dad, relinquishing the financial cushion granted by the lack of car payments along with the image of driving a flashy 911. When I thanked my father for the Porsche and showed him my new car, blood pumped through my heart and veins like a tidal wave. Sure enough, he was incensed and told me that I was irresponsible to take on a car payment. Standing in my power with conviction, I thanked him again, and then I softened to realize that behind his gruff exterior his motives were the same as mine. Deep inside, he only wanted to feel needed, lovable, and valued.

Meanwhile, a couple of years into my tenure at Orgdata, the company started to struggle. They brought in a new CEO to lead a turnaround. His name was Rhys White, and he came out of the high ranks at IBM. Separated from his wife and three sons, Rhys was single when he joined Orgdata. One evening when he stayed at work unusually late to close end-of-the-quarter business, he strolled into my office, sat down, leaned back, and put his feet up on my desk. His casual, friendly behavior made me nervous. I did not understand his intentions. Was he flirting with me? Was he like this with all women? Did he think I'd be fun for the night? Was he looking for a girlfriend? When he left to answer a phone call, I packed up my briefcase, ran out the door, and peeled out of the parking lot.

Relaxing at home in my bathrobe, I had just popped a baked potato into the microwave when the phone rang. It was Rhys. He asked me why I had left in such a rush, because he wanted to invite me to dinner. I played dumb and gave him excuses as to why I could not go out with him. But Rhys is the consummate salesman, and he did not give up until I said yes. Fifteen minutes later he was knocking at my door.

Our first night out was fun. He picked me up in a black Porsche 911. We went to a nice restaurant for dinner and then to a bar for drinks. We were comfortable and electric together, both passionately ambitious. Orgdata and our mutual history at IBM gave us a lot to talk about.

At IBM, romantic relationships within the company were highly encouraged, as they fostered a corporate culture where the workplace was your house, home, and family for life. At Orgdata, the ethic was flipped. For political reasons, manager–employee romance was frowned upon. As a result, when Rhys and I went public with the news of our relationship, it created a company-wide scandal. Rhys was labeled a skirt chaser. Coworkers accused me of spying for the CEO and aced me out of meetings. The head of human resources said the gossip surrounding Rhys was disruptive to the company and convinced me to leave with severance.

I was an outcast again, and this time it was serious. As a lone wolf with enemies, my livelihood was at stake. I had six months of severance to tide me over while I figured out if my career in Silicon Valley was salvageable or permanently sabotaged. For the first month, I cried alone in my condo and wallowed in sadness while my mind imagined a slew of demons and worries. When I explained all of my feelings and fears to Rhys, he assured me he was committed to our relationship.

Meanwhile, Silicon Valley circuit boards were lit up and hot with gossip. Rhys was seventeen years my senior, only three years younger than my mother. It turned out her best friend had a good friend who was best friends with Rhys's wife. One day my mother called to inform me that Rhys was not yet divorced. The revelation socked me in the gut. Young and naïve, I hadn't realized there was an important distinction between separation and divorce. Distraught, I called Rhys for clarification.

Even Rhys was unsure of the legal terms and the process. I didn't know if that made me feel better or worse. In all of the drama that was building, Rhys promised he would marry me as soon as he could, but I was not sure I could trust him.

Symbolically kicked to the curb as a gold-digging, social-climbing slut, I was stripped of income, identity, and security. I had no idea what to do and only a psychologist to guide me. The irony was that when I met Rhys, he was in debt. It was only after we started dating and working as a team that he began to earn big money.

Since Rhys was still legally married and the divorce was not happening, I pressured him on the time frame. I was not going to sit in my condo and wait for some guy to maybe marry me. So Rhys took me shopping, bought me a promise ring, and invited me into his legal process. At that point, the tables were turned. I chose Rhys as my mate and soul's purpose. My entire life and all of my energy became focused on him. I even negotiated his divorce with him and a team of lawyers.

When Rhys and I began dating, I was still referred to as a "big girl," because I was tall and curvy. It gave me confidence that he asked me out despite my full figure. After I left Orgdata, I had free time during the day and hired a personal trainer. He worked me out hard several days a week with rigorous cardio and weight lifting. The scale was my nemesis, so I did not use one. Unaware that my body was slowly transforming over a six-month period, I was surprised when people started telling me I was skinny. *What? Me?* It was surreal. Thirty years into my life as a "big girl," it was heady to suddenly receive compliments about my figure. With severance pay in my pocket, I went shopping for couture.

For the first time in my life, I felt good about how I looked and began to enjoy socializing. Every night Rhys and I went out to dinner, alone or with others. He brought me to all of his weekend, evening, social, and business engagements. Orgdata was an international company, and we began traveling the world together for business. After every meeting I wrote notes on index cards about each customer and their spouse so I would remember the personal details next time we met. I used a large recipe box to hold my cards in alphabetical order. The social skills I learned from my father and my in-depth understanding of Orgdata's business were invaluable assets to Rhys and the company.

Although Rhys was nearly two decades older than I was, his youthful energy and physical appearance belied his true age. We were always able to meet in the middle because I was ahead of my time. We even looked like brother and sister—two tall blonds with a strong presence together.

Raised in a midwestern farm town, Rhys was old-school and chivalrous. He opened car doors, house doors, and building doors for me and always insisted, "Ladies first." Best of all, he didn't seem to mind my moods. One time I asked him, "Why do you put up with me?"

Unlike my family, he cheerfully responded, "Because you always bounce back."

Rhys was my lifeline to the world. He got me out of the den and into the jungle. Socializing was a lot more fun with him as my partner. I never had to enter a party alone or feel rejected as a wallflower. He pulled me into all conversations, never left my side, and always spoke highly of me. In turn, I was his confidante who helped him endure. He made better decisions with my input and thrived with me on his arm.

Breaking off from my family was frightening, isolating, risky and painful, but in the end, I succeeded in finding my alpha mate. Rhys and I were in sync with ambition, raring to mark a large territory and lead a new pack. I didn't know exactly where I was going, but I had learned a lot about myself, possessed a lot more confidence, and felt better than I had since my childhood.

Chapter Six

alpha wolf mother

The soul is healed by being with children.

—*Fyodor Dostoevsky*

Wolf packs love puppies and rear them collectively with reverence. When the alpha mother is pregnant, she diligently selects and prepares the den. It is a sacred place and solely hers as she whelps her pups in private. After the birth, while she nurtures and governs the newborns, her mate provides her with food. Several days or weeks later, when she is ready to share them, she debuts the puppies to her clan and is met with a joyous serenade of wiggles, yips, and trills.

In January of 1992, Rhys and I announced our engagement, and my power began to stack up. Orgdata was rising, and Rhys was lauded as a turnaround hero in the Silicon Valley press. Earning good money, we bought our first house together, a mansion in the exclusive town of Atherton. Overnight, I became popular as fans came out of the woodwork: new friends, old friends, traitors, and strangers. Even former colleagues who had rebuffed me all of a sudden turned sweet.

Rhys genuinely loved parties and people, both for pleasure and for business. The connections were important to him. I, on the other hand, was more of an introvert who had always felt uncomfortable in groups. Rhys was my foot in the door and my anchor on the inside.

With him I was able to experience popularity. Moreover, given my work with the trainer, I finally looked the part, which allowed me to deliver a commanding performance.

When Rhys and I walked into a party, all eyes were on us. My ways were striking and mysterious. I put out just enough energy to tickle the crowd, and then I held back, creating a palpable aura around me. I liked to intrigue people and draw them in. At 6'2" in heels, I was easy to spot from a distance. My thick, long blonde hair was a beacon, and my new figure accentuated the couture.

Rhys was well known and electric. He led our way through the crowd with verve and bold confidence, networking adeptly with charm and good banter. Once he swooped in with the initial connection, I helped him expand the conversation and deepen the rapport. He was high-flying, and I was down to earth. Together we had synergy.

Although I didn't particularly enjoy the socializing, the newfound attention made me feel powerful. Most of all, I loved dressing up in beautiful clothes. High fashion was my fine art of choice. Awestruck by the many impeccable facets of haute couture, I marveled over the dazzling visions, original designs, intricate details, custom fits, and sensuous feel of the craft.

My entire wardrobe was visualized and coordinated by Risa at Neiman Marcus. She was a legend, performing miracles for her rich and famous clients. For fifteen years, she dressed me from head to toe, and we were very close. I spent hours every week in her private domain. It was an intimate, storybook experience to be in her parlor, as if I were Cinderella and she were my Fairy Godmother.

Risa's room was expansive and cozy, designed and decorated in style and for comfort. There was a couch, coffee table, desk, chair, fitting platform, and more. When I walked into her realm, a wall of mirrors greeted me with my own reflection. Quickly my eyes shifted to the abundance of splendid couture strung out in glory on rods. My mouth watered as I moved closer to the smorgasbord of luscious earth tones and rainbow colors. I gave in to the temptation of touch, running my hands over the finely textured garments. The smell of exquisite artistry was intoxicating. I became high on the fumes of creation.

Risa's court hummed as costumes and courtiers danced to the wave of her wand. There was often a knock at the door in between fittings while I was in my panties and bra. When it was Ansel, a young man from the shoe salon, she asked him to wait. "One minute, please. She's getting dressed."

After access was granted, Ansel slipped in, balancing a half dozen shoeboxes between his hips and his chin. Placing them all on the ground, he then gently unwrapped — one by one — twelve slippers, much to my delight.

Another knock at the door; it was the head seamstress.

"Inga!" I exclaimed. The babushka made me feel soft in her warmth as she pulled me into her short, strong, plump body. She was my once-upon-a-time grandmother with an old-world accent. Something about her made me want to be seated at her hearth listening to stories amidst the smell of warm bread.

"How is your family?" I asked with great interest.

Risa leaned into our exchange and waited for a pause. "Inga, please hem this dress about four inches above the knee. And give the side a little tuck with your pins. Let me see how it looks. Ansel, when you go back to the salon, please bring Lucinda a pair of Chanel two-tones to try on with the pink tweed Chanel suit. And see what you have to go with this silky black Escada gown. Oh, and bring those new strappy white Prada heels. I want her to try them with the Armani pantsuit."

Then — *poof* — Risa would disappear to return with an armful of purses, bags, belts, and coats. There were more garments too. For each piece that did not work, she brought in three candidates to replace it.

Risa knew the details of my full calendar six to eight months out. For every upcoming trip and occasion, my ensemble was acquired and ready to go in advance. For spontaneous invitations, there were plenty of options in my closet. I never had to wear the same outfit twice.

My wardrobe received a lot of attention in our social circuits. There were days when women went to Neiman Marcus asking for "the yellow dress with matching coat that Lucinda White wore last night." Remarkably, Risa knew most of the players in our various arenas. Even more impressive, she ensured my outfits were one of a kind.

Adorning myself with fabulous apparel was a thrilling and creative outlet for me, but it was also an important job, which I regarded as necessary to maintain my identity. Workouts with my trainer, suntans by the pool, cutting back calories, and blow-drying my hair straight were all key to my overall presentation. Sleeping was important too (when it was possible), along with highlighting my hair and waxing my skin. It's ironic that my father's training had finally fully kicked in, even though I had once rejected my parents' values. I had come full circle, demonstrating that life lessons happen in cycles with layers, and old habits die hard.

With my newfound confidence and image, the relationship with my parents began to heal. I had become everything my father had dreamed I would be, and it felt good to make him proud. This time around, it was my idea to be thin, pretty, and popular. That is who I wanted to be, and it was an important experience for me to immerse in that persona to know it firsthand.

In the month of August, Rhys and I were married in a quaint church nestled among a grove of redwood trees in Portola Valley. Immediately following the wedding, my parents hosted a reception for two hundred guests at their home in the same town.

Right away I dreamed of having a baby. I vividly recall my first home pregnancy test that turned positive. Ecstatic and overjoyed, I did a ten-minute happy dance in my closet. My heart had never felt so alive.

One week shy of our first wedding anniversary, Ella was birthed. Bright, engaging, delightful, and beautiful, she was everything I had dreamed of and more. Obsessed with child psychology, I did a lot of research and reading, and I attended a series of parenting classes with Ella from the time she was born until she was two. I wanted to honor her true nature and cultivate each level of her development. Every day was an exciting new discovery for me as I viewed life through her eyes.

Ella never sat in a stroller because I wanted her close to my heart. She came with me everywhere I went during the day, and our housekeeper, Consuela, was on hand to babysit when Rhys and I went out at night. To help care for Ella on the road, Rhys's mother, who lived in Illinois, traveled with us on business trips.

Two years later, our harmony came to an end with the birth of our second baby. As a mother of two, I was entering a new life season and my priorities shifted. Something inside of me longed to connect deeply and joyfully with both of my children. I wanted to be fully present and guide them as unique individuals until they came of age. Suddenly my glamorous lifestyle had less meaning and turned into a heavy burden.

I had no idea how to naturally evolve from one way of being to another. It seemed to me that women were not allowed to change. Instead they were expected to add more to their plates every year and strive to do it all. Eventually I would learn that transformation requires endings or death to create space for new life and beginnings. Until then I would remain immersed in dichotomy and struggle to stay the same person that others expected while responding to the yearnings of my authentic nature.

Jake was a sweet baby with a different temperament than Ella. While Ella had always been content to sit in her jumper and watch me shower or do dishes, Jake preferred to be held—and for good reason. He suffered from reflux, which caused him to vomit several times a day for a year. Born with an underdeveloped esophageal sphincter, he was not able to hold his food down.

Baby Jake also suffered from colic related to his disorder. At night I paced the house for hours with him crying in my arms. When he finally fell asleep and I laid him to rest in his crib, more often than not he would throw up all over his pajamas and sheets. After cleaning things up, I never knew how many more rounds it would take before he was able to go down in peace without getting sick again.

My baby was uncomfortable, and his condition was messy. As a result, I was not able to run errands, eat at restaurants, or travel with him. Rhys was gone much of the time, attending to business trips without me. Luckily, at home Consuela helped me a couple days a week.

The year that Jake was born Orgdata reported record revenues and a 60 percent growth in earnings. Rhys was on fire, at the peak of his career, but I was overwhelmed with the number of invitations we were receiving. With little desire or leftover energy to socialize, it was virtually impossible for me to keep up the pace with Rhys. But I tried.

One month after I birthed our son, Rhys insisted that we attend the San Francisco Symphony's opening-night gala with several of his business associates. I knew nothing about classical music, and I did not feel interested to learn. My ignorance made me self-conscious, and my hormones were out of whack, but somehow I managed to squeeze my postpartum body into a supertight gown. The seventy-five-minute ride to the city added to my discomfort.

Although Rhys knew most of the men at our table, I did not know anyone and felt it was my job to dazzle. Mustering my darling persona, I made it a point to engage with each person one at a time and dig deep for topics that they found interesting. Halfway into the dinner, I was caught off guard when my traditional role shifted and the wives began to nurture me. When they learned I had just given birth four weeks prior, they seemed surprised and genuinely concerned.

One of the women looked into my eyes and said, "Honey, you should have stayed home."

The feeling of validation and compassion she gave me was so rare that I burst into tears.

For most of my life I've had one best friend at a time, someone who is in the same situation as me: a college roommate, a boyfriend, or a coworker. I am intense. I like to focus and go deep with purpose into whatever I'm exploring at the time. And when there is no one "in it" with me, I go it alone.

For five years, Rhys was that person. He was my best friend and focus. Completely devoted to my man, his career, and his friends, I did not have friends of my own. While socializing with Rhys, I met a lot of women, but we did not get together one on one. My mother was close by, but our approaches to being a wife and mother were so at odds I found it hard and frustrating to speak with her about my problems, and I did not want to burden her. I'm sure she felt the same.

Without a confidante to help me sort out confusing issues and feelings, I slipped into another depression. This time my malady was different, because my babies were more important to me than I was to myself. I wanted to be present for them and forced myself to only express my apathy when they slept. Compartmentalizing myself, I allocated a specific time to be sad and reflect on my options.

Then, in the midst of my angst, a random impulse unexpectedly opened a door. I had always been interested in psychics, oracles, tarot readers, and alternative forms of medicine, but most people I knew thought it was hogwash. On a whim, I ordered a reading from an astrologer. I gave him the date, time, and location of my birth—that was it—and he mailed me a cassette tape with a one-hour custom reading about myself. We never met. We never talked. He had no idea what I looked like or if I was married. All he did was interpret my natal astrological chart.

The day that I listened to the astrologer's reading, which he referred to as "the blueprint of my soul," the floodgates opened. A force of emotion swept over me like a wave. But it did not crush me. Instead it *became* me, as if part of my soul were reuniting with my body. For years all my anguish, sorrow, and tears had felt like constriction and pain in my gut. This time the sensation was expansive in the area of my heart. As if I were my own long-lost lover, I wept at the sight of my true self and marveled that astrology could cut to the chase in one hour and know me better than five years of psychology did. I felt validated for who I was on the inside, and, amazingly, it helped lift me out of my funk.

What the astrologer said resonated. He gave me a new perspective on my life. One thing he told me is that I naturally had the vision, energy, and competency of five people. For decades I had worried that I was not good enough or doing enough. The astrologer's reading offered me an awareness that perhaps I am not spoiled and lazy, as I had often feared. He also said it would take an army of people for me to express my full self, and in that process I would elevate all those who were with me. He suggested I was a natural alpha leader who fosters and values every member in my trusted wolf pack. He said I would thrive—in work or play—leading a team of people with the principles of respect, cooperation, and deep connection.

Something deep down inside of me wanted to heal, grow, and strive for this new vision of myself and align with my authentic nature. I was dedicated to the children, Rhys, our livelihood, and our image, but I also wanted to carve out time for myself to continue the work I'd begun with Dr. Thomas. I had stopped seeing him several years prior, when my life was on a major upswing. It was as if I had learned all I could about the psychology of my earthly human nature. Now I felt called to explore the invisible nature of my soul. I was motivated to do it because I knew that all aspects of my health — physical, mental, emotional, and spiritual — were integral to my family's survival and success.

Meanwhile, in the face of my new revelations, our social invitations continued to mount, and I felt the pressure of it. My excuse for staying home — having a newborn — was getting older by the minute. Confused about how to sort out and act on everything that was swirling in my head, I continued to believe (as I was taught) that I should "do it all."

Haunted by my postbaby figure, I hired a new personal trainer. Wanting to make a proper comeback, I set an ambitious goal to debut a sleek figure at the fifteen-party holiday season, just four months after Jake was born. To support my expanding roles and responsibilities, I strengthened my pack by increasing Consuela's hours and hiring her daughter, Lela, to help me care for the children.

Wolves are synonymous with intuition, family, and wilderness. The truth is, something inside of me wanted to shapeshift. I had a feeling and a knowing that it was time to gracefully end one season of my life and move into another cycle of learning, but counter to that, I was conditioned to buck up, power through, and do more to prove my worth. If I didn't "do it all," I was worried my family and friends might reject me as lazy and weak. Growing up in a culture where invisible things were undervalued, I struggled to trust my intuition and honor my emotions. Without guidance or role models, I did not yet know how to voice what I was feeling and fully follow the natural stirrings of my soul.

If the soul is healed by being with children, then mine was on the mend. What I did not yet know is the child I most needed to be in touch with was my inner child, the part of myself that is authentic, soulful, wild, and free.

Chapter Seven

out of balance

We cannot be happy if we expect to live all the time at the
highest peak of intensity. Happiness is not a matter of intensity
but of balance and order and rhythm and harmony.

—*Thomas Merton*

Within nature's universal rhythm of chaos and order, there is no
such thing as good or bad. There is only in and out of balance. When
a wolf pack becomes too large, quite often their prey population will
decrease. If that happens, one of three events might follow: the pack
may attempt to take over another pack's territory and food source;
the pack may choose to self-regulate and abstain from breeding;
or nature will intervene to force a wolf reduction through famine,
weakness, and disease.

Humans, collectively and individually, have the capacity for expo-
nential growth, but when is enough enough? Is there not a time and a
place for everything, including plateaus, prunings, maintenance, and
rest? Rhys and I were brilliant partners, manifesting money, home,
family, social status, and pizzazz, but the rate of pushing forward
was so great I could not sustain it. My pack was growing, and good
things were happening. But what had once pleased me and fulfilled
me—being Rhys's business partner and trusted adviser—no longer did.

At the end of 1996, the year after Jake was born, Orgdata reached a high of 940 million dollars in annual revenue, and Rhys received NASDAQ and Emory University's Legend in Leadership award. The more parties we attended, the more people we met, the more invitations we received. Rhys said yes with pure joy to everyone and everything unless I doused the idea. At first I kept score and tried to balance my affirmatives and negatives, but my nos became the predominant force. With Rhys I only had to say yes once, but I had to decline ten times before he heard me say no. Having to say it so many times turned me into the "no person," and I felt guilty for being unsupportive.

In the beginning of our relationship, when being on the A-list was my only job, I felt powerful, popular, and lovable. But over time I became suspicious of false motives and bored with false fronts. I was a mother now, experiencing unconditional love for the first time. I wanted more of that.

For years I had been Rhys's business confidante, listening and offering advice. It felt good to know that he trusted and respected me in that way, but eventually I was spread too thin. It was not easy for me to draw the line, but my motherly instincts kicked in, and I left the business matters up to my husband. I felt something shift for Rhys at work when I redirected my energy to the children. Deep down I felt lousy for neglecting him.

In January of 1997, we moved to a larger Atherton estate, which doubled our land, square footage, and prestige. Our new home was more befitting of a prominent CEO like Rhys. The property was fenced and featured a call box where guests pushed a button to announce their arrival. If the visitor was approved, the front gates opened and cars rolled along a winding gravel driveway lined with tall trees. There was a second gate at the exit. We had a third gate too, hidden on a far side of the property. It was private, for family members only, so that our comings, goings, and parking of vehicles did not clutter the estate's well-groomed presence.

Venerable magnolia, oak, and birch trees framed our ten-thousand-square-foot, whitewashed-brick home and added to its old-world appeal. The gardens were lovely, with expansive green lawns, meandering box hedges, and a profusion of white iceberg roses.

Guesthouse, saltwater pool, koi pond, and tennis backboard — those were just some of the other amenities.

From the outside, the home was welcoming, soothing, gorgeous, and grand. On the inside it was enormous, barren, and cold. Rhys was traveling for business the week that we moved. On my first day there, alone with two toddlers, the movers were gone by dusk. They left me with four hundred unlabeled brown boxes scattered all over the hallway, dining room, and kitchen. I had no idea which box had the diapers, and there was no food in the fridge. Hungry, tired, and frightened, my babies clung to me as their cries echoed off the empty foyer walls. The three of us fell asleep on the floor.

In the following days, unpacking was all on me. Consuela did not speak English, and Lela was only part time. Overwhelmed, I had no idea where to begin. I was ground side on life's teeter-totter, weighted down with material obligations. Feeling depressed, I could not bring myself to unload the boxes. It was all I could do to take care of my kids.

Once again, my mother saved me, but once again I fought her every step of the way. Intuiting my depression, she called me every day and asked if she could help. Not wanting to burden her, I said no every time. One day she came over unannounced and found her way into the house through an unlocked back door. She told me about acupuncture and insisted I visit a practitioner she had researched. I was annoyed and told her I did not have time to visit a doctor, let alone drive thirty minutes each way. She offered to babysit and would not leave until I agreed. Graciously, she cared for my kids every time I had an acupuncture appointment. And she helped me unpack all of the boxes.

Heat was a physical issue that plagued me. My body ran hot, even in the winter. I always wore tank tops and never a sweater because my face easily flushed or broke out in a sweat. I had no awareness of why until the acupuncturist told me that my body's system was out of balance. He said I was using my inherent fire to accomplish a lot of work, but I had been exerting too much effort for too long. Like a car, my body was overheating. He encouraged me to find ways to relax and be more receptive, to balance my outgoing energy. He suggested I find ways to mimic the element of water, which is cool, moist, and receptive.

Working with my acupuncturist, I learned that my sadness and lethargy were messages from my inner self, clues that something was wrong. Sitting alone at home with my moods — and feeling them — was not pleasant, but the discomfort ultimately prompted me to expand my awareness, discover new perspectives, and learn more about myself.

My first depression had led me to psychology, where I learned about human nature. My second depression had spurred me to explore astrology, which informed me about the spiritual nature of my soul. And this third depression led me to acupuncture, where I learned about energy and the ecosystem inside my body.

Acupuncture offered me new concepts to contemplate and practice. As I consciously embodied the wisdom, my life began to improve. By slowing down and receiving, I gathered and regained energy. It was healing to let go of resistance to my mother and allow her to help me organize the house. Rhys suggested I increase Consuela's hours to match the scale of our home, and we offered Lela a full-time job as my nanny and assistant.

Lela was a godsend, a symbolic wife for me. Over the years, we enrolled her in cooking school and driving school and bought her a car. She was thrilled to learn new skills and take on increased responsibilities. With her help, my home soon evolved into a sanctuary centered around the children. The household and our schedules ran efficiently with ease, rhythm, and purpose. Rhys traveled and earned the money while I stayed home to manage our pack and estate. Grateful, I valued each member and their contributions to our whole. Organically, we connected and moved like wolves with a vitalizing energy that flowed through the cords of our heart-to-heart connections. Even though the pack was growing and our territory was increasing, I'd found a way — through acupuncture and increased support — to help my clan survive and thrive.

For a brief moment, I was back in balance, but I had not yet realized life is cyclical and to everything there is a season. I still believed that stasis was the ultimate goal, a static balance with no changes or ups and downs. Unforeseen forces would soon intervene to teach me more about excess, chaos, tension, and harmony.

At Orgdata, as president, CEO, and chairman of the board, Rhys was under increasing pressure to maintain the company's stellar momentum. At nearly one billion in annual sales, garnering relative ongoing growth was a substantial undertaking. Because it was a publicly traded company, the executives were required by law to forecast and meet accurate financial numbers four times per year. Predicting and achieving the actual results was a tedious quarterly game and a double-edged sword. Underforecasting relative to the previous quarters indicated a slowdown in growth, the kiss of death for a stock's price. Even worse, it could imply the executives intentionally lowballed their projections to manipulate a windfall with the final results. Overforecasting definitely suggested there was something wrong, because it meant the company failed to meet the expectations it had set. No matter how you sliced it, getting the numbers wrong at the end of the quarter was a red flag that would cause Wall Street analysts to issue a hold, sell, or do-not-buy recommendation. That, in turn, would spur a drop in the company's stock price. All of this affected customer confidence, future sales, employee morale, and executive job security.

Sure enough, in April, just three months after we moved into our stately new home, Orgdata announced a 140-million-dollar loss for their first quarter. It was big news and quickly triggered multiple class-action shareholder lawsuits. Overnight Rhys and I swapped fame with shame as the drama played out in the media for all to read day by day and blow by blow. Legal accusations, suspicion of fraud, shareholder anger, and pressure from the board of directors forced Rhys to resign by the end of July.

I was definitely scared and worried that people would think my husband was a crook, but Rhys assured me he had done nothing wrong. While Rhys and I had for years discussed business — the mechanical details of publicly traded companies, stock equity, shareholders, quarterly results, and lawsuits — we never talked about our feelings. Rhys was always upbeat and in charge, a glass-half-full kind of guy. Neither one of us knew how to have honest discussions about our deepest insecurities, regrets, and fears, which compounded my anxiety and interfered with our personal growth.

Rhys is an early riser. Every morning during the scandal he read the paper and marked it for my viewing. It was a harsh wake-up call that turned my stomach. I couldn't even drink my coffee. As I read the articles and talked to Rhys, I thought to myself, *do not panic.* But underneath my calm exterior, fingers of fear twisted my guts, and my heart beat staccato.

To this day, when Rhys feels blue, his fix is to go out on the town and be with people. I wanted to suck it up and help him recover by socializing and dazzling as if nothing was wrong, but I didn't have the confidence. The bad press triggered old wounds of being unlovable and rejected. I had no idea who I could trust, who genuinely supported us, or who was stabbing us behind our backs. My feelings were complicated and conflicted. I felt guilty and responsible for Rhys's scandal because I had stopped being his business sounding board, but I was also relieved to have a good excuse to avoid the social scene.

For months I stayed home in the silence and seclusion of my sanctuary with the support of my pack, only going back and forth to Ella's preschool. I did not talk to anyone — friend, family, or professional — about my feelings. For comfort, I began to dabble in self-help by reading spiritual books like *Women Who Run with the Wolves* by Clarissa Pinkola Estés, *The Mystical, Magical, Marvelous World of Dreams* by Wilda B. Tanner, and *Journey of Souls* by Michael Newton.

True to his style, Rhys rebounded much more quickly than I did. He did not care if some people feared and snubbed us. A senior executive in Silicon Valley with nearly three decades of extraordinary experience, he was immediately hired to help smaller companies. The timing was extremely fortuitous. It was 1997, the beginning of the dot-com bubble, when gobs of Internet-based companies were founded, creating very young millionaires and billionaires overnight. Every company that employed Rhys to consult or sit on the board offered him highly profitable Internet-boom stocks. Ironically, he made far more money after being ousted from Orgdata than while he was there.

Although many people shunned us and blamed Rhys for the fall of Orgdata, in 1998 the scandal eventually blew over and invitations to parties and dinners from old and new friends resumed. After nine or so months in seclusion, I started to rally. Rhys was chomping at the bit for me to accept invitations, and I was tired of feeling like an outcast. Ready to hold my head high and demonstrate with dignity that I stood by my man, I began to prepare for a comeback the only way I knew how: by commanding a beautiful and powerful facade and performance.

With many private parties, lavish galas, and other high-society events on my calendar six months out, it was once again a big job to acquire and manage my wardrobe and accessories. Although Rhys appreciated my striking appearance at parties, and maybe even took it for granted, he just couldn't comprehend how much it cost in time and money for me to keep up the image.

My feelings around money were conflicted. It was an uncomfortable financial adjustment for me to go from being an independent career woman to a housewife. I felt guilty for not earning the money I spent. But I also felt—now more than ever—it was my job to make a *big* impression.

To dress for my part, I continued to visit Risa in her parlor at Neiman Marcus. I still loved the experience and reveled in the luxury of freedom to afford couture, create fabulous outfits, and look good in them. It took hours to try on clothes and accessories. The process put me in a trance, but when the clock struck for carpool time, I jumped. There were kids to pick up, activities to orchestrate, dinner to be served, and bath time, bedtime, and story time to conduct. Pulled by the impulse of a mother, I would ask Risa to quickly wrap my purchases, but quite often I would have to dash out the door empty handed as Risa blew me a kiss.

There were many mornings when I woke up with dread because when the kids were at school I would need to carve out more time to go back for my costumes and props. Luckily, Risa was organized and the handoff was swift. We had a deep trust with each other. I'd not so much as glance at the prices or sign a receipt. And yet an ache gnawed at my stomach, because the purchase was always colossal. It often took two people to walk it to my car.

Driving home I was always full of anxiety as I worried how to unload my bounty. It seemed crass to parade such opulence before Consuela's eyes, and I was ashamed to subject my hardworking husband to the bills.

Scheming to hide the sight of my plunder became a drawn-out covert operation that filled me with dread. After sneaking the packages into my closet, there was much more work to do. First I made space for incoming items by creating a pile of donations. After I unpacked and put away all the new things, I had to sneak out heaps of hangers, bags, tags, plastic covers, tissue paper, and boxes. I worried about being caught discarding the evidence, and I hated the amount of packaging waste. And just when I'd nailed it and finished this cycle, special orders would arrive in the mail or Risa would call to tell me, "A fabulous gown just came in that will be perfect for the Black and White Ball. I'm holding it for you in the back. When can you come in to try it?"

One moment I flourished in the gifts of beauty and felt good for supporting my husband in his arena. But in the next moment, I felt shallow for loving the finer things in life and judged myself as a subpar housewife.

Adding to my discomfort around spending money, my extended family thought the best mothers did all their own cooking, babysitting, and cleaning. Anything less was selfish and unfair to the children.

I never did fit the cultural norms of a mainstream woman or a housewife. Nor did I feel appreciated for who I was on the inside. I tried to please people and fit in the best that I could, but it seemed no matter what I did and no matter how hard I worked, it was never enough. It only served to push me further and further out of balance.

Still disconnected from the balancing force of my authentic wildness, I was out of touch with rhythm and harmony.

Chapter Eight

the call of the wild

He had been suddenly jerked from the heart of civilization
and flung into the heart of things primordial.

—*Jack London*

When I had reached the peak of dedicating myself to material
achievements and duty, Wolf summoned me in a dream. Ethereal,
my body hovered low near the floor of a fairytale forest as a thousand
trees towered above me, dressed in beards of gray mist and billow-
ing capes of dark shadow. They seemed to be wizards gathered in
council. In the distance, we heard a haunting and alluring wolf call
that caused the hair on my skin to quiver. This vivid dream lingered
in my body like the howl of an ancient forest.

Dreams speak in symbols, the language of the soul. When we sleep,
our bodies communicate with a higher source, receiving a treasure
trove of wisdom and personal information to guide us through life
on Earth. Although I did not yet know how to interpret my dreams,
I had recently been inspired to write them down in a journal. By
simply recording them, the communication between my spiritual
and human self was enhanced.

Looking back now, I know Wolf appeared in my dream as a symbol
of my authentic wildness. Her hauntingly lonely howl was calling

me back to my original self. Excessively concerned with the tangible aspects of my humanness, I had neglected the invisible nature of my holiness.

Routines and order that had once grounded and soothed me eventually turned rote and bored me. Too much duty had tamed my spontaneous nature, doused my creative fire, and dulled my sensory perception. Wolf was the antidote for my domesticated life.

After the dream, Wolf followed me wherever I went. At the toy store I saw plastic wolf figurines. Advertisements for wolf documentaries popped up when I turned on the TV. On a trip to Wyoming, I was mesmerized at every turn by a barrage of wolf images on books, T-shirts, walls, and purses. When a poster for wolf-tracking expeditions flew off a bulletin board and landed on the sidewalk before me, the image of paw prints stirred me deep in my soul.

Wolf had my full attention now. I began to obsess—buying, reading, collecting, and watching everything and anything about Wolf. I fell in love with the details of this species: the fur, the howl, the pack, the hunt, the feast, the famine, their intelligence, and their sentient ways. The pull was steady. Wolf was my passion, my teacher, my guide.

When I researched the history and biology of wolves, I learned they were feared, hated, and hunted to near extinction in the United States in the early 1900s. It was excruciating for me to read about the wolf wars and look at the images of mass carnage. My knees wobbled, and I bent over in my chair to protect myself from the empathetic pain. With a heavy heart and streaming tears, I hummed a grieving howl for my kin.

Before I had e-mail or used Google search, bookstores were my best friends for research. When I discovered East West Bookshop, it changed my life by introducing me to an amazing new world. It was full of all things metaphysical: books, crystals, singing bowls, CDs, tarot cards, incense, talismans, and more. Guest speakers and healers held sessions in their classrooms on subjects including mysticism, dreams, animal augury, yoga, Jungian psychology, and life after death. I was inspired with every visit and stayed for hours perusing the shelves.

Guided by curiosity and bliss, I reveled in the freedom to browse without goals or rules. My body was loose and relaxed. Filled with awe, I wondered, wandered, and marveled as I absorbed the good energy

I intuitively felt. There was something about that place, something invisible I couldn't describe. I just knew that I liked the experience and was compelled to keep at it. The best part was at each visit, I was serendipitously drawn to certain books, trinkets, and tools that altered my perspective on life.

I found Ted Andrews's book, *Animal Speak: The Spiritual and Magical Powers of Creatures Great and Small.* In this encyclopedia of animal and bird symbolism, Andrews describes an animal totem as any animal a person feels closely associated with during their life. Like dreams, totems speak the language of the soul and link humans to the spiritual realm.

Before there were self-help books, psychologists, podcasts, and spiritual retreats, humans considered wild animals their best teachers for self-awareness. Animal totems helped and inspired people to heal and grow. They were respected as mirrors and guides demonstrating specific behaviors, strengths, characteristics, and skills for humans to emulate, as well as weaknesses to modify.

Ted Andrews got me thinking about human nature and the deeper meaning of life on Earth. It was then I realized, in retrospect, that my mom and dad's inherent natures resembled Lion's. That perspective offered me another layer of compassion and understanding to our relationship. Lions and wolves are equally magnificent predators, but they have different strengths, weaknesses, characteristics, and personalities.

Learning to see and experience the unique beauty in every animal and person has been a lifetime theme for me. Reading about reincarnation shed light on this when I learned that we all have issues to overcome and special gifts to offer the world and that each lifetime builds on the next. I now believe that souls come down from the spiritual plane to materialize as humans on Earth in order to learn, grow, evolve and contribute to making this world a better place. My body will die at the end of this lifetime, but my soul never will. Instead my soul will reincarnate in another body to build on whatever I accomplished in previous lifetimes, including this one. That wisdom offered me meaning and purpose, something everlasting to strive for. I was eager to discover what my soul wanted to accomplish, and I no longer feared death.

Metaphysical revelations excited me and spawned my desire to have deep philosophical conversations about the meaning of human life on Earth. No one I knew believed in this stuff, and I couldn't convince them to do so. I was trying to improve myself, but I had nothing tangible to show for it, and no scientific proof it was valid. Working alone, I stayed up late at night exploring new material and concepts. I sacrificed my sleep to be nocturnal like Wolf.

It was kismet that led Rhys, Ella, Jake, and me to visit our friends on their sixty-two-thousand-acre property in Montana just three months before my fortieth birthday and the turn of the century. The moment I walked through the front door at Kendra and Joe's ranch house, I felt a slight tug to my left. Instinctively I turned and saw a buffalo skull whose horns turned up toward the sky. Breathtaking! I was enraptured.

Never before had I been interested in bones, but this relic was magnetic. Pulled in closer, I inspected the skull in detail. Its triangular shape intrigued me, and so did the orifices. The circular eye cavities appeared to me as portals, and the nose cavities looked like tunnels, perhaps to another realm.

When Kendra said she had found it on their property, envy ripped through my gut. I wanted such a skull for myself. It must have been obvious, because she offered to take me to the place where the animal had died. Ecstatic over the possibility, I prayed there might be another.

The next day, her family and ours drove in 4x4s across gorgeous, rugged terrain. A rainbow of colors blurred as we drove by yellow wildflowers, green thickets, and a gushing blue river with white currents. Erupting on our path, birds painted the sky as we passed.

When we arrived at the site, my lips parted in awe as I saw a massive, thirty-foot-high cliff. It towered before us like an ancient altar rising from the dusty and barren valley floor. Exiting the vehicles, we gathered at the base, and Joe proceeded to tell us a story.

He said that millennia before European settlers arrived on the American continent, people on the plains used a hunting technique called *pishkun*, or "buffalo jump." Hunters caused a stampede on the high grounds, driving the buffalo over the cliff to fall to their deaths at the bottom where women waited to skin and process the animals for food, clothing, shelter, and tools.

The cliff wall—a buffalo graveyard that had been there for thousands of years—was polka-dotted with fossils and bone fragments compacted in dirt, gravel, and sediments of time. Right away I peeled off from the group, determined to find a skull before anyone else did. Combing the ground for fifteen minutes, I found nothing. When I looked up, I was surprised to see no one else was hunting for bones. The adults were standing in a circle drinking coffee, talking, and laughing while the kids ran around and played.

As if to tease me, some remnants of buffalo peeked out of the wall, while others were flush. Ravenous for bone, I let go of all modern dignity. Under the heat of September's sun, I went down on my knees and began smashing the wall. Shamelessly, I picked at what felt like cement with bare hands and a screwdriver as sweat dripped off my chin to my blouse. It had been decades since I had engaged in such uninhibited behavior, wild and spontaneous, without concern for the opinions of others. The rock face was a symbol of my mainstream armor, while quarrying wild bone reflected my quest to reclaim the lost shards of my soul. I was alone in a time warp, a madwoman on her haunches, desperately hungry for something familiar and primordial.

Jutting toward me at an angle, the cliff face was awkward and difficult to chisel, but I could not stop. Jabbing and tugging at one bone, I finally got it to wiggle. Two more jiggles and—SNAP—the bone came free. It fell into my palm, flailing like a live wire. Skin to bone, I curled my fingers around it and felt my blood go hot as an electrical surge fired up the DNA in every cell of my body. The flash ignited something primal in me, some kind of a memory. It felt as if I had known that animal ten thousand years ago.

Once the current moved through my body and I settled down, I inspected the six-inch bone. It was flat and narrow, very smooth to the touch, and pleasing to my eye. In surprising contrast to the stark-white bones I had seen in books and museums, the coloring of this one was warm, with varied earth tones of deep orange, red, and brown. One end of the rib had two protruding nodules. The other end was broken, revealing the catacombs inside.

Back home I looked up the symbolic meaning of Buffalo in my books and learned that this animal has an extraordinarily large body that is heavy, grounded, and rooted on the earth plane with the stability of a table on four legs. And yet Buffalo is also linked to the heavens through his horns that serve as antennae for communicating with spirits in the upper realm.

I then pondered the personal meaning of my encounter with Buffalo and intuited that he represented my need to remain present in the natural world while also reaching up to connect with divinity. Buffalo was a symbol, a vibrational medicine, talking to my soul. He appeared to recalibrate my body and help heal the imbalance of my mundane life.

Feeding me Buffalo for sustenance, Wolf called me back to the wild through my night dreams. Her long, arching bellow echoed from somewhere deep inside of me, rousing me like a lover's lament. My journey to Montana had been an initiation that reactivated a deep ancient connection to the wild animal kingdom.

After that, Wolf, Buffalo, and I were in constant communication as I continued to experience synchronicities, dreams, and epiphanies that guided my life.

Chapter Nine

animal speak

Bone by bone, hair by hair, Wild Woman comes back.
Through night dreams, through events half understood and
half remembered, Wild Woman comes back.

—Clarissa Pinkola Estés

At the turn of the century, Buffalo showed me that animals speak
to me the way my dreams do. Every animal encounter — dead or
alive, in dream or daytime — was an invitation for me to commune
with a mysterious force greater than myself. All I had to do was
answer the bid for deep connection with keen awareness. I began
to see the symbols, follow the tracks, feel the sensations in my body,
and intuitively interpret the messages. In a community where few
people understood me, animals became my sacred friends, teachers,
and allies.

Buffalo's rib bone was a talisman. I carried it with me in my purse
or my hand, and I placed it under my pillow when I slept, knowing
that we were in communion. In my research, I read that, symbolically
speaking, flesh is temporary and represents life on earth. Bones, on
the other hand, are regarded as eternal, like the soul, and never die.
Buffalo's bone had a tone that rippled and tickled and awakened my

own bones. Slowly and deliberately, it rattled and loosened memories that were buried deep beneath the surface of my awareness.

One day when I was outside in our yard playing with my young children in the rain, a trifecta of bone, water, and kids triggered a potent flashback to my childhood. As I saw myself swimming with the frogs in Oregon and then rolling like a fish in the river at Garr Ranch, my body recalled the feeling of bliss. I wondered why I had forgotten that part of myself for thirty years, denying myself such natural pleasure.

Standing in the rain with little Jake and Ella, I suddenly saw the juxtaposition of my two lives. Once a carefree, soulful, curly-haired nature child, I was now a materialistic overachiever who ironed her hair straight. Thinking of my children, I panicked to realize they were being programmed in Silicon Valley by a competitive culture that places a high value on academic degrees, money, fame, beauty, and intellectual (versus intuitive) knowledge.

That night I told Rhys, "We need a wilderness ranch."

He responded, "OK."

By spring of that year, we owned two.

The first piece of property we purchased was located two hours away in Carmel Valley, on a private preserve. Our lot was set amidst twenty thousand acres of pristine wilderness, and only two thousand of those acres were approved for the development of custom home sites and shared recreational areas like a horse facility and golf course. The remaining eighteen thousand acres were protected lands with green meadows, wild waters, and a lush forest serving as a wilderness playground and soulful sanctuary for the few hundred families who bought in.

At the center of the Preserve (as it's called) was a historic ranch house called the Hacienda that had been converted to an inn for members only. It had a restaurant, common area, and nine bedrooms. While planning a home for our fifty-acre lot, Rhys and I frequently stayed there.

The Preserve's outback set my soul on fire. I left the Hacienda alone every day and wandered through the ever-changing land-scape. Sometimes I followed the base of a canyon covered with thick walls of bramble and oak; other days I scaled a steep forest floor softly covered with thick redwood duff. Quite often my random glance would be rewarded with a bone, carcass, or feather. For each discovery, I screamed with pure pleasure and marveled at nature's bounty.

The other property we purchased was a historic orchard first planted in the late 1800s. It was located in my hometown of Portola Valley, where my parents still live, only a twenty-minute drive from Atherton. Nestled between the forested Santa Cruz Mountains and the town's main two-lane road, Finbarr Ranch was on the edge between wilderness and civilization.

When Rhys and I purchased the fourteen-acre property and saved it from residential subdivision, the orchard had not been farmed for more than five years. Trees were overgrown, and limbs were broken from the weight of unharvested fruit. A fallen oak with a ten-foot girth lay among motorcycle ramps carved out of dirt. Garbage—saved for a century—was strewn all over the place.

The debris had to be categorized according to specific recycling venues, and it took years of hard labor to methodically schlepp, lift, and dump it all. Sorting like crazy, we made hills of forgotten rubbish, half-empty paint cans, old rubber tires, and derelict cars. Along the way, we trimmed trees and smoothed soil, pouring our love into the land. Nurturing the environment, we became unwitting farmers, learning bit by bit in the process.

Engaged with all of my senses, I also became an earthkeeper, intuiting what the land wanted and working on her behalf. There is an ancient axiom "as within, so without," meaning our outer life mirrors the inner life of our personal thoughts and emotions. In tandem with my work at the ranch, I was clearing out the junk in my mind, discovering lost parts of myself, and nurturing my authenticity.

When I was at Finbarr, my inner and outer natures were intertwined and deeply connected. The ranch and I moved together in cycles and seasons, transforming ourselves on life's wheel of death and rebirth. When the ranch changed, I changed. And when I changed, so did she. In the coming years, there would be times I had to abandon her, and our separations led to illness. We carried it in our bodies with an eerie silence that manifested in drooping limbs, cracked soil or skin, and poor harvests.

I became a self-taught naturalist long before I knew what that meant. When I had applied for and attended college, the only degrees on my radar were business, economics, language, and history. At age fifty, it pained me to realize that I had never noticed or considered a broad range of outdoors-related degrees like forestry, botany, environmental science, or wildlife conservation. As I lamented and thought *that could have been me*, I eventually realized it was my blessing to be unschooled in the ways of nature.

My experience was personal, spontaneous, and genuine. Without a teacher, textbook, cell phone, or the Internet, I enjoyed the freedom of learning through random experience, trial, and error. Instinctive exposure to nature was healing, because I set my own agenda and pace. Once trapped in the dullness of too much duty and routine, I was now balanced by wildness, purpose, and bliss.

As I waded through weeds that reached my knees and I explored with dirt under my fingernails, I unearthed a plethora of animal bones—mostly deer. I discovered legs (femur, humerus, tibia, and radius), lower jawbones with teeth (mandibles), hooves, vertebrae, and ribs.

Deer is associated with the heart. Her medicine gently lures humans out of civilization and back into the wild nature of the forest. Feeling the soothing vibration of Deer's innocence influenced me to spontaneously operate from the love in my heart and to soften the sheer force of my overachieving will. In that process, her leg bones were there to symbolically hold me upright. Her teeth showed me how to chew on the cud of new perspectives and ideas; her vertebrae offered me backbone to move beyond the conditioning of false opinions and beliefs. And when I was ready, her jawbones encouraged me to voice the truth of my heart.

Immersing myself deeper each day into the naturally wild ecosystem, I witnessed our ranch as both larder and graveyard. Wild animals, insects, and birds gathered there to live, die, hunt, and be hunted in the great cycle of life. Each death was fuel for another life, and each bone was a reminder of the parts of our eternal self that never die. As within, so without. The bones were symbolic of my discovering and reclaiming the parts of my soul that had been tamed or rejected by social conditioning. Each bone was a symbol with a unique vibration that touched me deeply and moved me like a song.

If Deer is the most common sustenance for Wolf and we are what we eat, the symbolic nourishment of Deer bones was activating the disinherited Deer parts of my whole character. In daytime and nighttime, my soul was in dialogue with the symbols and signs of animals and bones. Wild at the ranch, immersed in new passions, I was following my bliss and at last reuniting with my authentically wild self.

Chapter Ten

owl full moon

It takes courage to grow up and become who you really are.

—*e. e. cummings*

Owl is a mysterious raptor who silently glides through the darkness on strong, broad, velvety-soft wings. Gifted with sharp vision and subtle hearing, she knows of all things that are hidden within the changing colors of night. By the moon's illumination or by the light in her eyes, Owl is able to see in the dark. A master of the nighttime, Owl is a feminine force who works in tandem with her shapeshifting sister, Moon.

Moon is receptive, creative, and moody, continually changing in contrast to her masculine brother, Sun. As Sun consistently shines in his full brightness, Moon continually waxes and wanes in a never-ending cycle of twenty-nine and a half nights. For two weeks each period, Moon's shape expands like a pregnant mother's belly, growing in brightness from a sliver of illumination into a full orb of light. For the last two weeks of her rhythm, Moon pulls her glow inward, gradually subduing until she disappears into the darkness, awaiting the rebirth of her next cycle.

In many native cultures, Owl is considered a bridge between worlds: flying through the ethers communing with Spirit and walking on the earth plane with two legs like a mortal. Revered for centuries as a spiritual guide and a messenger of wisdom, Owl's specialty is the feminine mysteries of Nighttime, Woman, and Moon.

Attuned by the buffalo rib bone and my time in nature at our two ranches, I felt the light of my feminine nature emerging from the darkness of my interior world. The Preserve was so ancient and wild it awakened all of my senses and opened me up to Finbarr. But the Preserve was remote and cumbersome to access, while Finbarr was nearby and easier to visit, on the edge where civilization meets wilderness. Over the years, I came to spend more time at Finbarr, learning how to synthesize different worlds.

Tapping into hidden parts of my soul with the help of nature, I was at last beginning to express my authentically wild self from the inside out. Owl showed up just at the right time as a totem to guide me on that journey. One afternoon as I wandered around Finbarr, I decided to sit and rest in the shade of a giant coastal redwood at the center of our property. Looking into her outstretched boughs, my mind soon drifted to thoughts of Julia Butterfly Hill. For 738 days Julia had lived high up in the canopy of a redwood she named Luna to prevent loggers from cutting the ancient tree down. Admiring the resplendent tree before me, I decided to name our tree Luna in honor of my heroine and our mutual love of all trees.

As I continued to daydream and look up to the sky through a pinwheel of long verdant branches, I noticed a caramel-and-white-colored barn owl nestled in Luna's arms. Gasping, I stood up to better see her. I marveled at her exquisite beauty as she perched on a slender limb, sleeping in full view. Intuiting it was a good omen to have an unusual daylight encounter with this nocturnal animal, I decided to name her Juju.

Observing Juju as she slept, I was inspired to spend the night in the orchard. I knew it would deepen my connection to the natural beings and elements at Finbarr. Waiting for summertime, I chose a date and arranged for Rhys to take care of the kids.

On a late afternoon in July, I arrived at the ranch, both thrilled and nervous to begin my mysterious nighttime solo adventure. As I unloaded my chair, mattress, and sleeping bag, I decided to set up my gear not far from Luna. I wanted to be out in the open, fully exposed to all of what nature had to offer.

Once my campsite was organized, I sat down to take in the view. A gentle breeze stirred the orchard, and I watched a family of deer feasting on fallen plums. I scanned the far end of our property where a mountain range rose from Earth's body like a woman's breast covered in a cloak of green. Taking in the splendid beauty, I felt the land — ever so slightly — rising and falling in breath. As Sun began to set, I watched his golden orb slowly disappear behind the ridge. Immersed in a crack between daytime and nighttime, I was moved to tears by the shifting at dusk.

As I glanced up to a purple sky, my heart fluttered when I saw the first star emerge. It reminded me of Garr Ranch when I laid upon the giant boulder as a child. Just as my mind flashed on an image of my grandmother Mimi, Juju flew out of the tree and into the darkness. Thinking about the synchronicity, I recalled that some indigenous people believe ancestors incarnate as owls to guide their human relations.

Much later, Full Moon shone silver above my head. Her light was so bright it illuminated the entire orchard, creating a shadow beside every tree. Night's breath was cool and damp. I lay awake in my sleeping bag and tuned into a nocturnal chorus of crickets, coyote yips, and the call of Great Horned Owl. I had not heard a hoot for thirty years, since my time at Garr Ranch. As the familiar voice landed in my heart, it echoed through my body, freeing fond memories of my childhood. Recalling my intimate rapport with kin and nature at Garr Ranch, I wept for the depth of my loss.

That night at Finbarr, I felt a myriad of invisible cords reaching out from my body to connect with the surrounding elements, animals, land, and plants. Our connections were conduits of communication transmitting energy and information to and from each other. From that point on, I knew in my bones that the ranch had a consciousness that recognized me every time I showed up.

After that night, as I returned to my daily routines at home, I found that my mainstream mindset had shifted. One thing I noticed was that every single summer camp that I knew of — for my kids and others — was highly structured. Whether the curriculum was billed as entertaining or academic, arts or sports, there were time slots for every activity, and children were told what to do, what to learn, when to take a break, and when it was time to eat. I had another inspiration.

Moved by the memory of Mimi and my time at Garr Ranch, I decided to create nature camps for kids at Finbarr, where learning would be spontaneous and guided by a child's internal curiosity. For the next year I daydreamed, set intentions, and made plans to launch my camps the following summer. Wanting my children to be with me, I debuted with a week for boys entering second grade and a week for girls entering fourth grade.

There were no set schedules at Camp Finbarr, just a lot of freedom to *be*. Kids ran, rested, jumped, laughed, and wandered. They were only guided by their feelings, moods, and whims. As an outward expression of what was surfacing inside of me, Camp Finbarr offered children what I needed to learn and remember. Together, the kids and I were returning to the primal essence of our original nature.

Most often, the boys arrived at camp in the morning full of vim and vigor and immediately set out to play. Sitting under Luna, I observed them naturally releasing pent-up energy by playing self-initiated games in the meadow. Wiffle ball, kickball, hide-and-seek, and capture the flag were their favorites. In contrast the girls regularly began their day by gathering in a circle under the boughs of Luna. After spreading out blankets upon which to sit or lie down, they chose basic supplies from a lineup of buckets. Sometimes they asked me to teach them a craft and other times they taught each other. We painted on rocks, knitted on knobbies, and wove friendship bracelets with beads, all the while talking and laughing. Afterward we often wandered the land to gather cattails, flowers, and leaves—and whatever else caught our fancy.

On hot days, longing to cool down with water, the kids took to the marsh. I was entertained for hours watching the girls romping and rolling in stinky warm sludge. Sinking into the succulent mire, they slathered each other in mud masks to soften their skin. The boys camouflaged their bodies with mud and then split into teams for muck wars. I was thrilled to observe their hunting stealth as they hid in the willows, crawled through thickets, stalked their prey, and flung mud bombs across the pit at each other.

When the kids were hungry, they foraged for blackberries, raspberries, and boysenberries. Or they climbed trees to pluck apricots, apples, and plums. As they gorged on the sweet flesh of fruit, orange, purple, and red juices dribbled from their fingers and faces. Inspired by the colorful liquid, they used nature's dye to paint signs on scraps of old wood.

Tapping into their primal nature and the thrill of the hunt, every day I wrote down riddles and clues on note cards and hid them all over the property. One card led to another, pushing the kids' edges and inspiring them to discover and know places they had never thought to explore. I tickled their brains with jokes, rhymes, and images that led them to treetops, wells, animal habitats, and abandoned man-made buildings. Observing the pack from afar, I smiled witnessing their enthusiasm for freedom and adventure.

Relentlessly following the tracks, signs, and clues, the little pack of hunters would ultimately find the honey-colored bandana, redeemable for treasures. Racing back to me at home base, they handed me the scarf, breathless and eager to claim their prizes. Extending the mystery, I asked them to sit in a circle while I drew their names out of a purple velvet pouch to determine the order in which they'd choose a talisman. Then slowly and carefully in silence, I pulled out a glistening silver key and unlocked a small antique wooden chest. As I invited the first child to come choose a hidden treasure, I tilted the box and opened the lid on its hinges for only him or her to see into. The other kids watched, wide eyed, as their friend's face glowed in the rays of magic emanating from the open box.

I traveled far and wide scouring specialty stores and trading posts, hunting for talismans to share with my campers. Every day the box was full of different treasures that reflected something from nature: animal beads carved out of gemstones, replica bear claws, deerskin medicine pouches, crystals, feathers, and porcupine quills.

Being around children and nature at Camp Finbarr reactivated my authentically wild nature and encouraged me to be more spontaneous and joyful in other areas of my life. Feeling a pull to do more of what I wanted to do instead of what I thought I should do, I immersed myself into the worlds of biointensive gardening, permaculture, animals, and wilderness education. The same year I debuted the camps, I took numerous classes, toured teaching gardens, volunteered as a docent at an environmental education center, and created a fifty-by-fifty-foot sustainable organic garden at the ranch.

Inspired by Mimi, who gardened with a cattle dog by her side, I adopted a blue merle Australian Shepherd puppy. As a bridge to my heart and the essence of Wolf, I named my dog Marga, which means "Follow the animal path to your innermost heart."

Over the next six years I went on to host summer camps, seasonal day camps, school field trips, and harvest-time farm tours. All the while, Wolf was my Earth totem, guiding my human personality and behaviors. And Owl was my spiritual totem, animating tracks, signs, and clues on my soul path.

Working with Moon, I was receptive, creative, and inwardly connected to the wisdom of my feminine nature. Working with Sun, I outwardly expressed my masculine energy to materially manifest my visions.

The year I launched Camp Finbarr was epic. It stimulated my internal light to grow. I was experiencing, firsthand, the difference between masculine and feminine, human and spiritual forces. But I had not yet learned how to bring them all into a natural balance and rhythm.

Eventually I would learn — through observation, immersion, osmosis, trial and error — how to thrive in a flow of dark and light, inward and outward movements. But first my Full Moonlight would abruptly turn dark, and I would be forced to face nighttime, darkness, and shadows.

Chapter Eleven

owl dark moon

God turns you from one feeling to another and teaches
by means of opposites so that you will have
two wings to fly, not one.

—Rumi

Barn Owl is lovely and distinguished with a heart-shaped face. She keeps rodents in check and the environment in balance. A prolific hunter, her favorite delectables are rat, mouse, lemming, vole, shrew, and gopher. Little stiff feathers frame her visage, designed to collect subtle noises and reflect them into her asymmetrically placed ears, for maximum efficiency of hearing.

Hiding in the dark, prey cannot escape Barn Owl. Her mind works with a complex web of sensory circuits that allow her to pinpoint and analyze all angles and frequencies of sound and movement in her landscape. With perception that is hyperacute, Barn Owl hears and feels the gopher rustling in his tunnel, the muffled squeaks of a baby vole, and even the slightest shiver of a mouse frozen in fear.

Owl hunts with her head, receiving holograms of information about her prey. Quickly discerning input on the fly, she performs a last-minute twist of her body to seize—with sharp talons on her toes—a creature lurking in the dark shadows.

Swallowing her prey head first and whole, Owl's body knows which parts to absorb for sustenance and growth and which parts to release. Within sixteen hours after her digestive system has sorted out the prey's nutrients, organs, and meat, Owl is ready to purge those things that do not serve her. After coughing up a firm pellet of bone and fur, she drops it on the earth for nature to compost.

After Camp Finbarr debuted, Rhys and I were both riding high on a new wave of personal success. My soul was blossoming through creativity and a connection to nature, and Rhys was energized by his work with fast-growing Internet companies and new restaurant investments. One evening, out of the blue, as we were driving to a pre-opening private party at our newest restaurant venture, Rhys took a phone call from his lawyer that he put on speakerphone. It was about Orgdata. The lawyer was somber, brief, and direct.

"I have some bad news," he said. "I just got off the phone with the US district attorney. Rhys, you've been indicted by a federal grand jury on eight counts of securities, wire, and mail fraud. The prosecutor will announce it to the press in the morning." He went on to say, "I'm so sorry, but I will make arrangements for you to self-surrender, so officials will not come to your house and take you away in handcuffs."

My heart dropped to my stomach, and I lost my breath. Fear swept through my body. As I felt pinpricks of terror under my skin, dark thoughts and words plagued my mind: *Bad. Failure. Publicity. Prison. Cage. Trapped. My children.*

After Rhys hung up the phone, we sat there in silence. Unsure of how much time had elapsed, eventually we looked at each other and recognized that the show must go on. In autopilot mode, we parked, walked across the street, put on our game faces, grabbed each other's hands, stepped onto a terrace, and opened the door to another realm. Once inside, as if we didn't have a care in the world, we hosted and dazzled a hundred guests in honor of our newest restaurant's opening.

Late that night after our event, we talked about the indictment. Full of conviction, Rhys assured me once again he'd done nothing wrong. He was eager to fight it and prove his innocence. Although I never doubted him, I had issues. I worried about what other people thought of Rhys, our children, and me. And my Wolf nature had a deep-seated fear of the cage. The thought of prison terrified me.

After we finished talking, I sat silently, anticipating and dreading the onslaught of bad press and gossip. Five years prior when Rhys left Orgdata under suspicion of fraud, I was embarrassed. But at least it was an *accusation*, not a charge, and its power diminished when I thought the incident had blown over. This time around, I recognized it must be far more serious than I had ever imagined if a grand jury determined there was enough evidence to put Rhys on trial. Once again, my childhood wounds, fears, and insecurities came flooding back.

With only a few hours to prepare before Rhys's story hit the papers, my number-one priority was our children. This time they were in grade school, and the bad press could affect them. I decided not to talk to them about what was going on. Legal matters are technical and complicated. How could I explain indictment to small children when I barely understood it myself? I would wait to see if any kids on the playground said something about it to them. Ella or Jake would let me know.

In the meantime, my strategy was to be proactive and honest with the adults who mattered most to my children. Instinctively, I knew if I stayed ahead of the media with those people, I could reduce surprise, confusion, questions, and gossip that might filter down to the children, theirs and mine. That evening I prepared and sent a simple, straightforward e-mail to the parents of my children's closest friends and to their teachers and coaches. I outlined Rhys's situation and thanked them in advance for helping to support and protect our kids.

Yanked from my bliss and thrown into fear, my Full Moon expression abruptly turned dark. Although I had done a great deal of work to improve myself over the years and possessed a certain level of self-awareness, the indictment triggered unresolved issues related to my self-worth. Weighted down with worry about negative publicity, my family's survival, and the uncertainty of Rhys's future, my wings felt clipped. As both guide and mirror, Owl would soon appear to reflect that state back to me.

On one of those first days when we were dealing with the indictment, Chase, our ranch manager, called to tell me he had found a dead owl, shot under the wing. My heart stopped as I thought of Juju. I prayed it was not her and shivered to imagine her shooter and his gun. Tight in my chest and short of breath, I jumped into the car and floored it to the ranch.

The first thing I did was visit Luna to see if Juju was there. Relieved that she was, I stood there in gratitude. Then I headed to the apple barn where Chase had put the dead owl for safekeeping. I paused outside the door for a moment and imagined the building was an Egyptian mausoleum. When I stepped over the threshold and entered the room, Owl's presence was piercing. I had never been that close to a raptor.

Cradling the owl in my hands, I gazed at her face in silence and took in the details of her majesty. Stilled by her awesomeness, I felt light and receptive, as if I were absorbing her essence. She was a barn owl like Juju, with a white heart-shaped face and a round head. Her beak was curved and sharp under eyes that were glassy from death. Her caramel-colored feathers were soft to the touch like the finest organic spun cotton.

Intuitively, I closed my eyes in homage and said thank you to Owl for gracing me with her presence. Acknowledging the sorrow in my heart for the trauma surrounding her death, I assuaged my grief with a loving prayer. In that moment, a warm breeze lightly brushed the hair on my arms and head, as if her soul were swirling about me.

Placing her on the table, I spread her wings wide and took in her supernal beauty. A spot of blood drew me in, and I inspected the wound. Daydreaming, I realized that with a clipped wing she had not been able to rise, glide, or hunt through the ethers, which caused her to die on earth's plane of existence. Feeling a resonance with the dichotomy of her earthly and soulful natures, my eyes welled up with tears.

Wondering what to do with her body, I stood quietly and waited to receive inspiration. When an idea came to me, I followed it. Without full understanding of what I was doing, I cut off her wings and her feet to preserve them. Setting them aside, I gathered the rest of her body and went outside to dig a proper grave. When I was done, I laid the owl's body inside Mother Earth and then placed the palms of my hands over her body. Closing my eyes, I expressed my gratitude to receive her medicine, guidance, and wisdom, and then I imagined a bridge of light to assist her soul's travel back to her home in the heavens.

That evening I brought her wings and feet to my office in Atherton. I was astounded to realize they were symbolic of my eternal soul and my temporal humanness. Even more telling in hindsight is that the two large wings were folded, and her eight toes, capped with dagger-like claws, were curled in. Naïvely, I placed them on my antique leather-lined bookcase, unaware there was meat under the skin that would naturally decompose with bacteria, insects, and mites.

White-collar crime was on everyone's lips in 2002. At every dinner, party, and event, the daily headlines about Enron, WorldCom, Tyco, and Martha Stewart were discussed in jest and disdain. While people were talking, I could not help but wonder if their judgments and jokes were directed at Rhys and me. I could not conceal my discomfort. At the mere mention of corporate greed, crime, or prison, I felt the unbearable strike of a match. It lit the base of my spine like a fuse that raced to my skull and ignited my face with red-hot shame and dripping sweat. I could not control it, not even when I wore tanks tops in winter.

Many people and groups dropped or blackballed us. One day a woman called to tell me her husband was going to rescind an invitation he had extended to Rhys to play in a golf tournament with him. He was worried that his association with Rhys on the golf course might taint his image and thwart future business opportunities. She agreed with her husband's concern but was sorry for the predicament and wanted to give me a heads-up. We also received hate mail and phone calls from people who had lost money when Orgdata's stock dropped. One anonymous letter read, "You reap what you sow." And a friend of my birth family called to tell me that my husband was a crook.

Fortunately our children were fine throughout the drama. When I had more clarity around the process, I was able to tell them briefly, with a strong and calm demeanor, what was going on in the moment and what might come in the future. I let them know it was a very difficult situation but also an opportunity for all of us to learn and grow. My honest and direct voice, combined with support from the families I had initially contacted, ushered them through many years. I never heard stories or saw evidence of their being shamed or shunned by their peers.

Rhys and I were in this together. We stood strong for our family both inside and outside of our home. We talked a lot about practical matters related to the legal proceedings, but we did not know how to share our deepest feelings and insecurities with each other. If I was angry with Rhys, I was not consciously aware of it. He was the one facing prison time, not me. Or so I thought. Ironically, I *was* in prison, trapped in the deep, dark thoughts of my mind. Feeling guilty by association, my identity, image, and power were in question. I was vulnerable, scared, and ashamed to admit it.

For over a year, the legal posturing and proceedings on Rhys's case were played out in the media for public awareness and fodder. Although Rhys wanted a trial to prove his innocence, the sentence could be up to five years in prison if a jury convicted him. I was gravely worried a jury would not be sympathetic to him, considering the national tension surrounding corporate fraud. Focusing on that, I urged him to settle with a plea bargain that could possibly lead to a lesser sentence. Succumbing to my pressure, Rhys eventually pleaded guilty to one count of criminal securities fraud.

At Rhys's hearing, the judge sentenced him to two months at a minimum-security federal penitentiary. Although sixty days was a godsend compared to five years, it was still physically, mentally, and emotionally daunting to prepare for his incarceration. There were a lot of legal issues that required attention, and a stack of documents to read that oriented us to all of the procedures, policies, and rules around inmate check-in, etiquette, phone calls, visits, and check-out. I also needed a power of attorney and complex training to stand in for Rhys in his absence so I could manage all of the business, financial, and legal matters that he normally handled.

Rhys was ordered to surrender on a specific date in September of 2004. That morning we left by car with a generous head start. His check-in time was very specific, and I didn't want to blow it, but as we got closer there was heavy traffic and the directions were confusing. By the time we found the road to the final destination, my stress was full-blown.

Flustered and tender, I was ill-prepared to see a guard tower with armed men sitting high above fences topped with large rings of barbed wire. Even though our lawyer and the paperwork assured us that Rhys would be serving time in a minimum-security prison, somehow, we were unexpectedly approaching a medium-security penitentiary. The blunt force of that surprise felt like a punch in the gut, but I had to keep rolling. With every turn of the tires, the sight grew more and more ominous. My heart pumped fear through my bloodstream, as I imagined a thousand violent criminals jumping the fence and storming our car.

As I pulled into the parking lot at the foot of the tower, a guard shouted down through his megaphone, "Pull over and park to the left. The driver is to remain in the car while the inmate approaches the gate."

I was so scared that my brain could not process the information. *Did he say left or right? What if I make a mistake and they punish Rhys for it?* My entire body was shaking as I looked for a legitimate parking spot. With all eyes on us, there was no time or space for proper good-byes. Rhys hugged me briefly and exited the car alone. I watched with anxiety as he approached the giant eerie jaws of prison. Sliding open and then closing quickly, the bulletproof doors swallowed him like Moby Dick. At that point, I was unsure if Rhys would be transferred to a minimum-security prison, or if there had been a mistake and he was incorrectly admitted to a much tougher joint. The logistics and duration of his "process" in that perilous place were unknown.

Still shaking from the whole of my experience, I desperately wanted to sob. In a flash, I thought the guards might disapprove, so I left promptly with good manners. Imagining I was under tower surveillance, I mustered all the adrenaline I could to focus on driving exact speed limits, staying inside the lines, coming to complete stops, and making proper turns. My measures were grueling until I finally found a safe place to pull over.

Walmart never looked so good. Sitting in my car on the fringe of a parking lot, I heaved tears from the depths of my soul. Empty, I left the asphalt asylum and headed out for my long ride home.

For nearly two decades I had been working on self-discovery. I knew my shadows, insecurities, and fears. But I had not slain them yet. Feeling once again like an unlovable outcast, I also began to see that I was ruled by the opinions of other people. By letting their personal judgments, beliefs, and perspectives define my self-worth, I was disrespecting my own inner voice of authority.

As devastating as it was, my predicament was an opportunity for growth, and I knew it. Studying and observing Owl's behavior, I was inspired to sit patiently in my darkness to hunt for the pestilent thoughts that plagued me. Owl wisdom guided me to grasp those pests, discern my inner truth, digest the sustenance, and spit out what no longer served me.

As I turned from one feeling to another, I was learning through opposites and finding my two wings to fly.

Chapter Twelve

turkey vulture

People living deeply have no fear of death.

—*Anais Nin*

Turkey Vulture thrives in the realm of decay, kissing death on the lips with her beak. What others experience as ugly, putrid, and repulsive, Turkey Vulture knows to be beautiful, fragrant, and alluring. Feeding on earthly carrion, she cleans bones and inhibits the spread of disease.

Turkey Vulture is a raptor, but not a predator. With a keen sense of smell and vision, she is drawn to perishing flesh. Red and raw with no feathers, her head is unusual and perfectly designed for digging into rancid carcasses. Known as the "golden purifier," she keeps health and disease on the earth plane in balance by cleansing what is rotten.

At every sunrise, this queen of the sky performs an awe-inspiring ritual of reverence to the purifying nature of Sun. While she stands in a glorious horaltic pose with wings spread open six feet wide, Sun warms and dries her feathers of dew and disinfects residual bacteria. Enlivened by her lord, she soars and circles on thermals and currents for hours, searching for the newly departed.

Although Rhys was only gone for two months, it seemed like two years. I was lonely, and it was awkward to be out in public. I prayed no one would ask me "Where's Rhys?" And I wondered who was whispering "Her husband's in prison." True to form, Rhys made the best of his time. He found relief in the simplicity of it and was fascinated by the people and their challenges. I often wondered if I had a harder time than he did during those sixty days.

One day at the ranch, I noticed a kettle of turkey vultures flying low over my head. Curious, I watched them glide, dip, and circle until they landed behind some trees on the other side of the creek. Grabbing my binoculars, I moved in closer to see what they were doing. As I crossed the bridge, I could see they were feeding on a deer. Keeping my distance, I sat on a rock for an hour and watched them rip and tear at decaying flesh. Later that evening, I went down to inspect the deer carcass and noticed that Turkey Vulture had left me a gift. It was a fifteen-inch black feather from her wing.

From that day forward, every time I wandered in nature, I found animal parts in all manner of decay and purity. Out of the blue, I would feel a light tap on my shoulder or an ever-so-slight ping in my stomach causing me to inadvertently glance sideways or change direction. And then in a split second—POP—the sight of a dead animal or animal parts stopped me firm in my tracks.

I was a magnet for bone, feather, antler, and carcass. The variety I discovered was astounding, from a petrified jack rabbit head to a fully furred coyote tail to a paper-thin desiccated snake in the shape of an S. His protruding spine looked like a Slinky shrink-wrapped in dry skin.

Animals and their strewn parts became symbols, mirroring and revealing pieces of myself that were buried deep in my subconscious. As I became more aware and open-minded in nature, with a sense of wonder and joy, my collection was growing exponentially. But it was becoming an increasing challenge to find more space to store my treasures.

Our house was divided into two parts—formal and casual. The sumptuous half of our home was far too fancy for my comfort. A grand foyer, classical-revival antiques, hand-painted textiles on the walls, and a lot of rooms made it a spectacular place for large parties. But in all the years we lived there we only entertained in that area twice.

Neglected and lonely at the end of a long gallery, the living room seemed like a good spot to store my growing panoply of animals and animal parts. At first I tucked them to the side so my family and household workers would not see them, but over time there was no way to conceal my rapidly growing collection of cured animal parts, bones, and taxidermy that covered the floor and spilled out from tabletops, drawers, and couches.

Rhys was not bothered by my new obsession, per se, but he would have preferred I host people in that room instead of dead animals. As for my kids, they had their own interests and hardly noticed my stash. I felt strange hoarding animal parts in a proper Atherton mansion, but the dichotomy in the room was a fascinating reflection of my inner life.

At social engagements I was dying to talk about bones, but there was rarely an opportunity for me to gracefully slip in "Hey, I found a deer skeleton today and brought it home." One time I did boldly blurt it out, longing for someone to respond, "Really? Tell me all about it!" or "I love deer bones too!" But that did not happen. Instead I was met with puzzled expressions, scrunched up noses, and silence before the conversation turned back to business, politics, gossip, and who had the coolest kids.

My initiation into the transformational process of animal decay happened the morning I went to retrieve the barn owl feet and wings from my leather-lined bookcase. I was horrified to see only feather shaft, claw, and bone. I quickly did some research and learned about tiny moths and other microscopic decomposers that eat meat, skin, and the feather veins. That lesson taught me to put all of my individual feathers in the freezer for a few weeks to kill off any invisible scavengers. For fully feathered wings, I was inspired to make an incision in the skin and gently scrape off the meat with a razor blade. After I dusted the remaining moisture with cornmeal or salt (much later I learned Borax is better), I sewed up the hole. And when I found mammal bones with small remnants of meat on them, I soaked them in water and bleach to strip off the flesh and kill germs.

Fascinated by the decomposition of dead animals, I scoured the Internet but found very little information. Although I hired a taxidermist to preserve and stuff some full-body and shoulder mounts for me, he was not very helpful when I asked him questions. We had different interests. Taxidermy is the holistic art of arranging skin, but I was compelled to delve under the surface to dig for bones and examine decay.

Assuming I was the only person interested in this activity, I worked alone. Learning through trial and error, I used my intuition and experimented with salt, cornmeal, Borax, bleach, cold water, boiling water, sun, soil, horse manure, and hydrogen peroxide. Each technique had its pros and cons. Quite often my approach was dictated by the size of the animal or part and the amount of meat I needed to transmute.

One day I found a dead coyote on our property and immediately thought of Clarissa Pinkola Estés's book *Women Who Run with the Wolves*. I remembered her story of La Loba, which is about a woman who pieces herself back together in a process of searching for wolf bones. After she painstakingly finds and articulates a whole wolf skeleton, she begins to sing over the bones. Miraculously, the animal comes back to life and runs freely into the woods. As the wolf jumps over the river and catches a glint of sun on its back, it morphs into a fully fleshed and wholly whole wild woman.

Since there had been no record of a wolf in California since 1924, I sensed working with Coyote as Wolf's little cousin was my best chance to deepen my healing journey and reclaim lost parts of myself, but the logistics were tricky. I would have to deconstruct Coyote before I could reconstruct her.

Known as a shapeshifting trickster, Coyote was the perfect guide and subject for me. Shaped since I was eleven from the outside in, I longed to flip that process and express myself from the inside out. My challenge was how to get at the bone.

First I would have to figure out how to get Coyote's fur, skin, and meat off of her bones, but none of the techniques I knew were suitable for an animal that large. Waiting to receive insight, I sat with Coyote in silence. Filled with awe to be up close and personal with the majesty of her wildness, I scanned her body from head to toe. Her honey-colored fur with black streaks was long, coarse, and puffy. Her fluffy tail was thick and pointed at the tip like soft-serve ice cream. After counting her sixteen toes with chocolate-brown claws, I placed her front-right paw in my left palm and imagined her trotting on soil. Last of all, I gently strummed her highly tuned whiskers to feel her vibration ripple through my body.

Committed to preserving all three hundred bones and articulating her skeleton like La Loba, it came to me that I should leave Coyote outside and let the natural elements work on her. Knowing her parts would be vulnerable to scavengers, I asked Chase to build a protective fence around her body.

Coyote worked on me for over a year as I diligently tracked how the sun, shade, water, hot and cold air, soil, maggots, bugs, moths, birds, and detritivores interacted with her fur, skin, organs, and meat. Captivated by the process of decomposition, I was astounded to witness how death fed the ecosystem, reflecting the circle of life.

Around this time, I started noticing roadkill everywhere I went. The sight of bloodied animals splayed out on hot asphalt nagged at my stomach. I wondered if other people noticed or even cared. A week or more later, I'd wince each time I recognized the same creature, now steamrolled flat like paper by countless hasty cars. To witness animals dying a thousand public deaths felt horribly disrespectful. It was as if their lives were no more than trash.

Tortured by the sight of animals killed by cars, I began to pull over, jump out, and quickly move the body to bare earth, under a bush if possible. Before rushing back to my car, I visualized the animal's soul returning to heaven on a bridge of light, and I prayed he or she felt comfort in my gesture.

With every encounter, my passion increased, and I upped the ante. It happened on dark nights. It happened on freeways. It happened in Manolo Blahnik heels. One time I was driving on a narrow and busy winding road when I saw a beautiful skunk on the center line. My stomach became nauseous at the thought of ignoring her, but I was late for an appointment and the road was precarious. For ten minutes I agonized, and then I turned around to get her. With no shoulder for parking, I left my car at the mouth of a fire lane and waited for a lull in traffic. Running down the road in flip-flops as fast as I could around blind corners, I prayed no car would come at me. When I finally saw her, I quickly reached down, grabbed her by the tail, and raced back to the fire lane where there was more space.

Of course she smelled, but I didn't mind. With a sweaty face and pounding heart, I took three deep breaths, gently placed her under a bush, and then blessed her with a prayer.

Somehow word of my respectful ways spread quickly throughout the animal kingdom. Ailing and elderly birds, reptiles, and mammals came to die at my doorstep or sent out tendrils of energy to ensure that I found them. My relationship with every animal was intuitive and creative as I connected with the unique features and characteristics of each species and the varying conditions of their bodies. In sacred rapport, I blessed each animal by expressing my love and gratitude.

As I sat in silence, inspecting and admiring their features, I intuited when an animal wanted me to harvest a specific part of its body to be used as a symbol or talisman that worked like a dream and spoke the language of my soul. Tails helped me to restore balance, claws offered me protection, fur encouraged my use of intuition, and any piece could offer me a connection to the animal's spirit. When I was done, I left the deceased animal out in the open as food for scavengers, or I dug a hole and officiated a solemn burial with crystals, flowers, herbs, and water.

My relationship with dead animals offered me the intimacy I had yearned for all of my life. I loved the animals unconditionally, and I felt their love in return. I loved the animals in their fullness, no matter how seemingly ugly or putrid. Humbled to be under their skin and inside their guts with bare fingers, I was working through all layers to arrive at their bones. Finding bare bones represented my quest to reclaim lost parts of myself, and working with decay reflected my process of transforming belief systems and ways of being that no longer served me. With Turkey Vulture medicine, I was changing and purifying myself so that something new could be born.

Chapter Thirteen

raccoon

To be yourself in a world that is constantly trying to make you
something else is the greatest accomplishment.

—*Ralph Waldo Emerson*

With her distinctive masked face, Raccoon is part heroine and
part villain. She is a shapeshifter venturing into dark nights. Clever,
curious, agile, and dexterous, she delves into nooks and crannies
searching for sustenance. Disparaged by some for sifting through
garbage, stealing pet food, and raiding human homes, Raccoon is
beloved by others as a beautiful furry creature with anthropomor-
phic traits.

Raccoon has five toes that look like long fingers on each of her
four feet. She can open a jar, untie a knot, twist a doorknob, and
manipulate tools with her front paws, which resemble human hands.
She is a highly adaptive animal wonder who can survive in the city,
suburbs, or wilderness. She's a mate, a mother, an adventurer, and
an explorer. Fierce and sweet, independent and social, Raccoon has
many skills and personalities.

When I turned forty-eight at the end of 2007, I looked back and
dubbed it the year of Raccoon. At every turn, I had found her body—by
our pond, near a tree, on trails, and in the road. Stumbling upon

Raccoon twelve times in twelve months reflected the magnitude of my assorted personas. In her mirrors, I was able to recognize myself with compassion, and became more intimate with the process of death.

At every chance encounter, I sat down with Raccoon to let her know she was not alone. Assisting her transition, I prayed her soul would return to the spiritual realm with ease. Diving deeper into rapport, I faithfully cherished her body as I inspected its state of decay. With full presence, sincere gratitude, and sensory circuits wide open, I created connections that fed me information from a higher source. Deeply touched in this extraordinary way, I came to feel like a midwife of death, ushering souls back to heaven and transforming bodies to a new state of being.

Attending with all of my senses, I was able to intuit what to do with the bodies. Every raccoon was unique and requested something different. Some I buried in the underworld of dark, moist soil. Others I left where I found them, to feed life on earth. Three of them were mostly bone, which I cleaned up with hydrogen peroxide and then displayed as art to honor Raccoon essence. One was large and decaying. I buried her near my house and dug up her clean bones one year later. Another suggested I harvest her striped, furry tail to remind me of balance.

Nine raccoons later, I found two that were fresh and pristine. I took them to my taxidermist, who cleaned, stuffed, and mounted them in climbing poses on fallen tree branches. The twelfth raccoon was dismembered. All I found was her head, frozen in time. Miraculously her skull had retained its fur, ears, and whiskers, which was unusual. Typically the fur falls out when the flesh begins to rot. I suspected the natural elements magically conjured a rare and perfect recipe of temperatures and conditions to preserve her masked face for me. Looking battered, beautiful, furry, and fierce, with snarled lips and bared canines, it appeared she had departed from the earth plane with grit.

My Raccoon encounters were like night dreams symbolically guiding me in daylight. Each animal represented one of my various personas: socialite, nature-camp director, school volunteer, mother, wife, domestic, kid chauffeur, bohemian, and so forth. Through the lens of Raccoon, I began to notice my masks and how each one of my characters had a specific motivation, intent, and costume. Some overlapped, and others were polar opposites, creating dichotomies within and without.

There were periods in my life when I felt joyful and flexible expressing different aspects of myself, but for decades I had also created and amassed false fronts that were draining. Continually shapeshifting myself to please my family, friends, and the dominant culture was a never-ending job I could no longer sustain.

Adding to my workload, responsibilities, and personalities, for the previous three years, Rhys and I had also been managing a massive construction project at the ranch to build a near replica of the original farmhouse, a workshop for Rhys, and a studio barn for my assorted animals. Recently completed, we finally had a home at Finbarr and planned to stay there for summers and holiday breaks.

In tandem with preparing our new home, I organized my new barn. It was the most blissful and satisfying activity I had ever experienced. Awestruck by the beauty in every detail of the animal forms, my existence in the barn was timeless. When I arranged the animals as sacred art, there was no right or wrong way to do it. There were no rules to tell me how. And no one could do it better, because no one I knew had animal bones and parts.

Shed snake skins, deer antlers, opossum skeletons, and fox skulls came to life with my attention. In their presence I felt something palpable move through my bloodstream. I didn't know it back then, but the barn was a symbol of my heart; in the barn I was enlivened by love.

As the decades passed and my life grew more complicated, I'd felt something sucking the life-force out of me. Yet when I handled the bones and lovingly arranged them, I felt the opposite, as if they were breathing a life-force into me. The experience was not something I talked about in public; I had no words to explain the intangible. Best case, I thought people would consider me lazy, doing something unimportant, unproductive, and silly. Worst case, I worried they would perceive me as macabre.

As soon as the house was ready, we spent every school break at the ranch: Easter week, Memorial Day, summer, Labor Day, Thanksgiving, and Christmas. When it came time for us to clean, pack, and move back to Atherton, it took three cars to fit our stuff, the dog, and four people. Waiting until the very last minute, I cried every time I left. Finbarr had become me, and I it. We were one in our seasons and moved through the changes when we were together. Each separation threw me out of sync with the rhythms of nature and triggered a deep feeling of loss related to my childhood, even though Atherton was only a twenty-minute drive away.

Although I felt blessed to spend time at the ranch, my life was not synthesized. It was depleting to compartmentalize myself and zigzag back and forth among all my personas, trying to meet everyone's (sometimes conflicting) expectations. It wasn't clear to me at the time, but I was having an identity crisis. I could not decide if I was an aristocrat, a hippie, or a magical being. Was I the wife of Rhys White, a societal clone? Or was I me, myself, Lucinda? And who was that?

The year of Raccoon, was also my last year of three as PTA copresident at my children's junior high school. Miserable and trapped in that role, I asked myself why I chose to put that mask on. Normally I would have said "no thank you" to a full-time volunteer job with a long-term commitment constrained by obligations, regulations, and bylaws. But when I was nominated I said yes because Rhys had just been sentenced to prison. Fearful I would soon be an unlovable outcast, I thought a prominent leadership role in the community would secure my status and power. My ego took charge and sacrificed a big part of my soul to assume that false identity.

Related to my interior struggles, for many years a chronic skin condition had been smoldering under the surface of my right cheek. Highly sensitive to touch, food, topical products, and heat, the skin on my cheek was thin, shiny, and red. Seeking relief, I had tried facials, homeopathic remedies, acupuncture, modified diets, shamanic ceremonies, muscle testing, skin-patch testing, biopsies, topical and oral prescriptions, and more. Nothing helped. In fact, every approach and product caused a severe reaction and further aggravated my cheek until finally in 2007 it erupted and turned into a staph infection. From my chin to my eye and my nose to my ear, the right side of my face burned red with oozing blisters.

It would take many years for my cheek to finally heal. In the meantime, I never wore makeup, and sunscreen had the effect of acid on my skin. As if my bright-red cheek was not embarrassing enough, the high-powered dads on the sidelines of competitive youth soccer games teased me for wearing a goofy king-sized visor.

Taking a clue from Raccoon, I knew my cheek was a lesson about which face I presented to the world. Ever since I was a teenager, I had suppressed a strong resentment for being judged, liked, loved, and shamed for the measure and state of my external beauty and achievements. Decades of smoldering anger had finally bubbled to the surface and marred my face. No mask could hide me now. Unable to fall back on my good looks for power and acceptance, I followed the signs before me to symbolically interpret the underlying cause of my dis-ease.

In the dream realm, skin is symbolic of protection, and in ancient spiritual traditions the right side of a body represents our masculine nature. Reflecting on these symbols, I intuited a dominant force of masculine energy—both inside and outside of me—had burned a hole in my right cheek. I was severely out of balance, and would need to experience more of my feminine nature to heal. Rising above my personal pain, I recognized that the taming and shaming of my womanhood was a microcosm, reflecting a collective wound in the dominant culture.

Certain that my soul had a higher purpose to fulfill in this lifetime, I began to realize that I was not a victim of my afflictions: instead, my afflictions were my destiny to experience and resolve. I had to live them and feel them in my body to know them before I could reconcile them one at a time. I was developing strength, compassion, and wisdom so that someday I could help other people mend the same wounds.

One midsummer night, sitting outside under a full moon, enjoying a new level of self-awareness, I reflected on how I might stand in my power and shine fully from the inside out. I recognized if I wanted to be self-defined, not other-defined, some of my personas would have to die to create space for my divine feminine nature to emerge. Determined to reveal my full value as a woman—beyond the dominant cultural norm—I declared my intention to become a spiritual feminine elder, deeply connected to the source of all life on earth, serving the highest and greatest good.

Looking up to Full Moon, I asked her to show me the way.

Chapter Fourteen

autumn

She looked like autumn, when leaves turned and fruit ripened.

—Sarah Addison Allen

Time and life lessons are cyclical. Modern people often perceive life as a straight line thrusting forward into the future when it is actually circular, spiraling through thirteen moons and four seasons that revolve and recur every month and every year. Hence, time is a never-ending continuum comprised of three primary phases: life, death, and rebirth.

Mother Earth and her celestial Moon are simpatico, transforming in continuous rhythms. Every twenty-nine and a half nights, a new crescent moon is birthed from dark skies and grows into a full moon for approximately two weeks. Once peaked, the moon wanes for two more weeks until its light disappears into the womb of darkness to prepare for another cycle.

Springtime and the new moon are akin. Growing sunlight, fertile soil, and plant buds herald that spring is here. Swelling into the season of summer, sunlight peaks at the solstice, like a full moon. Deep-violet blueberries bursting from emerald-green stems and vibrant flowers in full bloom signal that summer is alive. Waning in light, autumn is a time to harvest with gratitude and share the bounty resulting from the work of previous seasons. Finally winter, like the dead moon, brings endings, rest, and repose. Animals hibernate, deciduous trees lose their leaves, and dimmer days grow cold as the darkness gestates new life to emerge in spring for another round of earth seasons and moon cycles ever after.

Like the moon, the seasons, and my collection of decomposing animals, my body was changing too. Although I had beautiful visions of becoming an elder ever since I was a young child, I was not prepared to feel the promise of menopause rumble through my body. Hot flashes, grumpy moods, tender breasts, dry eyes, and a dry vagina took me by surprise. I thought maturing would be easier, because I had wished it. Instead I felt overwhelmed by my flailing emotions, bombarded by the mass media's unflattering view of aging, and lonely for women who would engage in positive conversations about menopause.

My lessons related to womanhood reflected the cyclical nature of time. Learning about myself was never a linear process, instead the lessons kept circling back to test my resolution and ultimately offer me clarity through many layers of experience. By the time my PTA term ended, I was perimenopausal. That's when Lela retired to start her own family, and I regressed. Taking on the additional shopping, cooking, organizing, driving, and cleaning left me little time to feed my soul.

The next four years were brutal. I struggled to express my authentic wildness under the heavy influence of domestication. When Ella graduated from high school in 2011, I was hanging off a cliff by my fingernails. Adding to my malaise, my doctor told me I was postmenopausal because I had not bled in over a year. In a flash, my life season turned from summer to autumn without honor, awe, or ceremony.

After settling Ella into her freshman year of college, I was desperate to fill the void with new life, so I researched the deeper meaning of eldership and menopause. Listening to myths and stories from ancient indigenous cultures, I learned it was the elders who fed the souls of their people with wisdom. Hence, the older ones were needed, respected, and revered as the glue that kept their communities intact.

In my process of discovering the power, beauty, and value of aging, I also learned about ancient matriarchies that worshiped female deities. Their holy trinity was a triple moon goddess that represented the three primary phases of a woman's lifetime on earth as Maiden, Mother, and Crone. In these cultures, a woman's body was venerated as a sacred vessel in each stage of her life because it held the potential of creation and the mysteries of blood.

Menses means month and moon, reflecting that women are inextricably linked to the moon through their monthly menstrual cycle. A maiden who bleeds resembles the new moon. She is potential, new beginnings, growth, and fertility. Maturing into her fullness as a mother of children, nature, and creative projects, she governs sexuality, birth, and the energy of a full moon. In the third phase of her life, when a woman turns to autumn and her body begins to wane, she withholds her menstrual blood to make wisdom instead of a baby. As a sage woman, she is the balsamic crescent moon, the one who holds the mysteries of death.

Recognizing the healing powers of the moon so late in my life, I wept for the magnitude of my loss. In my maidenhood and motherhood phases, I had been deprived of experiencing my natural feminine rhythm. Spending much of that time powering through and forging ahead, I overexerted my masculine nature. I did not know the moon was my mirror, reflecting my divinely feminine, creative, and transformative ways. Unaware that it was essential for my body to synchronize with the moon's twenty-nine-and-a-half-night cycle, I disconnected from her wisdom and cadence by consuming birth-control pills for a decade. Further disrespecting the moon, the feminine, and myself, I cursed my period every month for nearly forty years.

Researching the wisdom of indigenous cultures, I stumbled upon a shamanism workshop offered at the Esalen Institute in Big Sur. Starving for like-minded people and out of balance from neglecting myself and tending to others, it was shamanism that grabbed my attention and lit me up. Fascinated, I wanted to pursue the adventure, but it was a radical departure from my normal routine. I had been with Rhys for twenty-two years and had never traveled alone or with friends, only with family members.

Scared as hell to take the leap, I mustered the courage to ask Rhys if I could attend the workshop. Saying the words out loud felt like an initiatory act. Rhys was surprised that I wanted to go away for a week by myself and even more taken aback when he learned where I was going. Counter to our luxurious five-star family vacations, Esalen had a no-frills, bohemian vibe. Although he was a bit caught off guard and confused, Rhys reluctantly said yes and confirmed he was available to take care of the family and homestead.

As the date drew nearer, I began to fear the unknown. Would I fit in? Would the accommodations be comfortable? Would I miss my family? Would my family survive without me? Unable to sleep, I felt in the pit of my stomach that I no longer wanted to go.

Rhys was not used to taking care of the kids for an extended period of time. Even though Jake was the only one at home and he was a teenager, Rhys and I were both nervous about my leaving. He did not understand why I was going, and I worried he would let something slip through the cracks. Being a control freak, I took several days and many hours late at night to gather supplies, prepare lists, consolidate contact information, and outline blow-by-blow instructions for Rhys explaining how to care for Jake, Marga, the house, and the comings and goings of our wolf pack. There were carpools to drive; school events to attend; soccer gear to wash, pack, and keep track of; games to witness; after-school activities and homework to navigate; parents to coordinate with; meals to plan and prepare; a dog that needed exercise; and more.

On the eve of my workshop, just as I had finished organizing and packing, a woman from Esalen called to tell me the class had been cancelled due to an emergency with the instructor. She gave me two choices: a full refund or another workshop. At first I was elated and thought, *This is a miracle. Hallelujah! I have an out, with a refund.* But my conscience stepped in. I remembered how hard it was to get to this point. I had approval from my husband, support for my son and dog, and five pages of action items typed up and taped to the refrigerator door. This was a test of my conviction to step out of the mundane and into the mystery. I could not back down. I said yes, but the only workshop with openings was titled "The Courage to Be You." I had no idea what I was getting into.

Waking up the next morning to gray autumn skies, I felt a tightness in my chest and those telltale pinpricks under my skin. Not wanting to leave my family and home, once again I fantasized a million reasons to cancel. Yet somehow I loaded the car and took off.

Luckily the drive was calming, lyrical, and soothing. Highway 1 in Big Sur is a serpentine road high on the edge of cliffs above the Pacific Ocean. Rolling around the curves, my breath lifted and lowered, tuning into the sinuous rhythm.

The setting at Esalen was equally spectacular. Long and narrow, the property was laced with tall ancient trees and spanned a lengthy bluff overlooking the ocean. A river from the mountains cut through the land, feeding the sea. Raptors, songbirds, and migrating monarch butterflies graced a brilliant ecosystem of organic edibles, aromatic herbs, and fall flowers.

Esalen is a place that encourages respect for nature, simplicity, community gathering, and room sharing. The accommodations are rustic, sparse, and mostly one-room studios with multiple beds. There is no cell service, Internet, or television, and guests are encouraged to bring earplugs to buffer the sounds of snoring.

I loved the simple lifestyle integrated with nature. The subdued minimalist lodging, in contrast to a fancy hotel, did not faze me. It was the people that triggered my discomfort. I arrived at the cafeteria a bit late for dinner. The room was already full, and the tables were jam packed with large groups of people completely engrossed in conversation. As I stood alone in the middle of the dining room with a tray full of food in my hands, my heart started to race. I scanned the room, flushed and self-conscious. It felt like sorority rush.

There were only a handful of open seats scattered throughout the room. I picked the one closest to me, which happened to be full of kids in their twenties. When I squeezed onto the bench to sit down, the table went silent. After a few lukewarm introductions, I realized it was an employee table. Surely they were tired from working all day and were eager to enjoy their young friends. Kicking into my darling persona, I tried really hard to make conversation and win them over, but it did not work. It was all-around awkward for everyone.

Way outside of my comfort zone, I wanted to cry and go home. At Esalen I had no power or identity. I was not Ella and Jake's mother, my father's daughter, or the wife of Rhys White. I was not a powerful socialite, nor did I know who I was without Rhys by my side. The feelings of rejection and not fitting in that I felt when I was single came flooding back to me. Aware that life lessons are circular, not linear, I knew the Universe had presented me with an opportunity to peel back another layer of the onion.

The opening session of our workshop happened right after dinner. There were fifteen women and two men, all ranging in age from twenty-one to sixty. It was clear from the introductions that we were all dealing with major challenges in our lives, including divorce, illness, physical abuse, and identity crisis.

Right away without warning, the teacher asked us to silently choose a person that we wanted to approach. It was required, not an option. And then she said, "When I say go, I want you to immediately get up and walk to that person to see if it is mutual."

Imagine a room full of people, each one making a beeline for someone who is making a beeline for another. Three people pounced on me so quickly that I never had a chance to move or to choose. All I did was look up and touch the one who had a split-second lead. Synchronistically, she was the woman I had in mind to target. At first I was stunned, then uplifted and happy, to finally be chosen, but immediately my heart sank to my stomach as I felt compassion for the two who had missed me. Watching other people wander the crowd in search of connection, I saw many parts of myself in the room.

Of course everyone adjusted on the fly and ended up with a partner one way or another, but I was very uncomfortable when the teacher had each one of us tell the group in detail who we targeted, who we ended up with, and how it made us feel. Many participants admitted their fear of rejection, and some talked about choosing several people who, one by one, turned away to another. I was amazed to witness their vulnerability and raw honesty. In my world, most people worked hard to project and uphold a perfect image, which required them to hide their true feelings, insecurities, and emotions. Finally, I was experiencing a realness in people.

Another exercise had us sitting cross-legged facing a partner and holding their hands. For five minutes each, we had to look the other person directly in the eyes and tell them — without stopping — all the things about ourselves that we felt were shameful and embarrassing.

All the while, the teacher roamed the room and eavesdropped to ensure everyone fully participated. With no time to think, my good-girl personality kicked in, and I obediently followed the teacher's instructions. After I blurted out a long list of unflattering insecurities, experiences, and weaknesses—eye to eye with a stranger—my body shriveled and my face turned bright red! Feeling naked, judged, and unlovable, I wanted to die from the intimacy and exposure.

It went like that for five days and nights as our leader presented an arsenal of intense and intimate exercises that triggered fears, tears, insecurities, and anger. I was dazed and confused, thrown onto a minefield of buried emotions, each one waiting to explode upon touch. She was not there to coddle us. Her mission was to help us get unstuck. She intentionally kept us on the edge, in a state of discomfort, in order to break down our social fronts. There was no way to be pretty and perfect. There was no time or space to compete. I felt overwhelmed by the onslaught of exercises and the turbulence of my own issues. Surely I was not alone.

On the first night, at the end of our session the teacher asked, "Is there anyone here who has not bathed in the Esalen hot tubs?" Five of us raised our hands. Knowing the baths were nude, co-ed, and open all night, I had no intention of tubbing it—not naked with men. But the teacher asked for volunteers to "take the newbies to the springs and show them the ropes." She said, "The tubs are intimidating until you do it one time. So just bite the bullet and go with these women right now. Take off your clothes, and get in." My heart lunged from my chest to my throat and beat so fast I could barely breathe.

The tubs were situated at the top of a cliff with spectacular views of the sky and the ocean. The first thing we were guided to do was strip down in a co-ed alcove and then rinse off under the adjacent showerheads. Once done, we each grabbed a small towel and followed our leaders to a pool. Luckily the people were friendly, and the dark moon obscured the details of naked bodies.

For more than six thousand years, the Esselen Indians and others have used the springs for ritual and healing. In the Esselen language, the springs are referred to as "the god in the waters." Slithering down into the lush, balmy liquid, my skin felt something ancient, familiar, and medicinal, as if I had done this before.

Purified in the water of Mother Earth's womb, I was initiated on the path from motherhood phase to wise woman. Deepening the ritual's influence, Moon was balsamic that night, a slim waning crescent, just as she was at my birth, fifty-two years prior.

The next day, as we dove into our class exercises, I connected deeply with several people. One in particular, a twenty-seven-year-old woman named Lucie, reminded me of my younger self. She was intelligent, hardworking, and beautiful, with a master's degree to boot. We paired up for several activities and felt very comfortable together. I learned that Lucie was an only child who had struggled her whole life with an emotionally unstable mother. Her stories were heartbreaking to hear. Several times I watched her tremble, held her hands, and felt the ripples of her deep-seated pain roll through my body. At the end of the week, we exchanged numbers.

The year following my Esalen experience, Lucie and I were in constant contact. She genuinely wanted to transform and was craving connection with elders. Lucie worked hard to discern and pull threads from the wisdom I shared and then wove them into her life. Within four years, of her own volition, she divorced her husband, sold most of her possessions, retired from a mainstream career, traveled the world, and met a wonderful young man. Knowing that I was an ordained minister, she asked me to officiate their wedding. One year later, they birthed a beautiful baby boy. Her transformation from wounded maiden to joyful mother was astounding and well earned.

Women need other women for stories, transition, support, ritual, and ceremony. Young women need elder women who are wise in their bones to listen, hold, and guide them. Older women need younger women, full of dreams, to honor the depth of their wisdom. Lucie was the first person to recognize me as an elder woman with invisible gifts. By the light of a waning moon, I saw who she was on the inside, and she saw me.

Stepping out of my comfort zone to attend a random workshop at Esalen was a bold move that shook me to my core. That leap of faith thrust me through a symbolic transition to my life's autumnal season and introduced me to people with whom I resonated. I was forever altered. By taking the risk, I opened up exciting new opportunities for myself.

Chapter Fifteen

wolf tracking

When we track, we pick up a string. At the far end of
that string a being is moving . . . [and] the animal's
movement is still contained in that track.

—*Tom Brown Jr.*

The image of wolf paw prints pressed on white snow is primal,
harkening back to a time when our hunter-gatherer ancestors considered wild animals their kin and evolved by modeling their behaviors.
Observing the hunting and survival skills of wolves, our forebears
learned how to track prey with all of their senses.

Wherever they go and whatever they do, animals leave a trace.
Remnants of fur snagged by a twig, old or fresh scat, foliage slightly
compressed, and the wet print of urine are signs of animal activity
and behavior. With keen observation and strong intuition, any seeker
of a connection to animals can read their signs and patterns.

Visible, tangible spoors hold a wealth of information. It's possible
to know by reading the tracks and signs the approximate day and
time of an animal's presence and where he or she was going. The
tracks might also reveal if the animal was walking, playing, feeding,
hunting, or being hunted—and even if he or she was calm, courting,
pregnant, or stressed.

Spiritual trackers know how to create a telepathic connection. They are able to feel the animal's body, heart, and soul by imagining their own hands and feet inside the animal's paw prints. In this way, tracking wolves becomes a metaphor that echoes the ancient way of hunting animals for sustenance. Wolves, as predators who hunt and eat prey, can teach a modern tracker how to seek food for their soul.

Atherton is a place where people drive around town in fancy cars and often do not know their neighbors. It's a suburb full of walled-in castles on large lots, majestic trees, and streets with no sidewalks. About one hundred years ago, it was the place of second homes for high-society San Franciscans who wanted a country retreat away from the hustle, bustle, and fog. Near the end of the last century, most of the estates were knocked down and rebuilt as primary homes for the movers and shakers of Silicon Valley.

When my children were teenagers, Marga and I walked every night along the sleepy streets of Atherton under both light and dark phases of the moon. Never did I see another person on foot until several years into my walks, when I was surprised to cross paths with a family of nightwalkers. The dad, wearing a headlamp, pushed two children in a stroller. Their dog trotted along by his side. Marga and his dog barked at each other, which made it kind of impossible to stop and chat. We yelled hello from across the street. Our mysterious and brief encounters left me wanting to know more about this unusual Atherton family.

Then one afternoon, shortly after returning from Esalen, I was out on a walk by myself when I was struck by the sight of a woman with wild and curly brown hair walking toward me on the other side of the street. Her Patagonia clothing was different. It felt earthy compared to the slick Lululemon daytime attire I often saw around town. Keenly observing her from afar, I recognized her dog. As she drew near, I felt a large smile rise from deep inside me. Without apprehension or thought, I introduced myself. Incredibly our connection was effortless as the conversation naturally flowed, heart to heart.

Her name was Delilah, and it turned out her family had been living one estate down from us for six years. As we wondered aloud how it was possible we had not known of each other before, we both confessed we felt disconnected from community and out of place living in such a haughty town.

I told her about my recent trip to Esalen, and she told me about her recent trip to a wilderness-living school in the state of Washington. She described it as a place where people thrived in harmony with each other and nature. She learned the old ways by making fire with friction, foraging for wild edibles and medicinal plants, building a shelter with local materials, cooking with natural techniques, and stalking wild animals. She had even learned how to trap and hunt with primitive tools. Her story captivated me. My heart longed to learn the ways of our ancestors.

Two days later, I found a handwritten letter from Delilah in my mailbox. She wrote, "Let's go on an adventure together! In the meantime, here is a long list of books about deep nature connection and native cultures that I know you will love." She also referred me to a handful of wilderness-living education centers, online classes, and teachers. I devoured the suggested books in a matter of weeks and hired Robin Russell, one of the teachers on her list, to privately mentor me according to the old ways of being.

Then Delilah called me out of the blue one day to tell me about a seven-day wolf-tracking expedition that was being offered mid-February in the Northwoods forest of Michigan. "Wanna go?" she said. Straight to my heart, the significance of her invitation caused me to gasp. Suddenly light as a feather, I dropped to my knees and tipped my head forward in humility. After a few moments of silence and awe, I heard Delilah's voice say, "Can you hear me?" Lifting my chin, I screamed, "YES!" and I thought to myself: *Oh my God. This is it.*

Electric, alive, and happy, I was one step closer to Wolf. My life felt sacred, as if I were being guided by something greater than myself. I knew it in my bones. Something big was going to happen in Michigan. As if to validate that I was on track, an important story hit the media. On December twenty-eighth, my fifty-second birthday (just one month before going wolf tracking), a lone wolf crossed over the Oregon border into my home state. It had been eighty-seven years since a wolf had been documented in California. I cried at the magnitude of this good omen.

The wolf, nicknamed Journey, had been collared and tracked on his long and lone arduous quest for a mate. Traveling through three national forests, Siskiyou, Umpqua, and Wallowa-Whitman, he finally made it to Lassen National Forest. I interpreted the news like a dream; it was clear that I was crossing into new territory for a rebirth. California reclaimed part of her authentic wildness the day Journey put his paw to her soil, and the story forebode my parallel journey to Michigan.

Under the pull of a very bright waxing moon, Delilah and I took flight. On the verge of a wild-woman adventure, we were free to let go of the domestic duties that weighed us down. The journey was twelve hours door to door, and we talked the entire time.

Arriving at the nature education center late in the afternoon, we had one hour to relax and unload our bags. Our room was simple, with two bunk beds and a desk. We brought our own sleeping bags and pillows for bedding. Shared bathrooms were down the hall.

Just before dinner, we gathered for a meet and greet. There were four instructors and seventeen participants. The group was hardcore. Most of the guests were avid and experienced young male and female trackers who had lived according to the old ways in remote areas of the Northwoods for extended periods of time. A handful of hotdogging outdoorsmen from Manhattan who had come to the woods for a wild and crazy good time rounded out the group. Not savvy with snow or tracks, I was clearly in over my head. Even Delilah had tracking experience. But I was game.

Wolf sightings in the woods are rare. Finding a wolf track in the vast wilderness requires experience and time. Even those lucky enough to discover fresh tracks might never see a wolf, because remote observation is difficult in a dense forest. As one might imagine, wolves are keenly aware and leery of humans. They sense our presence and remain elusive.

To give our group a leg up, every morning at early sunrise our leaders scouted the edge of the woods by car, hoping to discover fresh tracks where one wolf or more had entered the forest. If they were successful, our group's quest was to follow any tracks laid out before us in order to feel the essence of Wolf. Following the trail, we were to imagine the animal, what it was doing, where it was going and why. We understood that the ultimate, most intimate opportunity would be for the tracks to lead us like the pull of a string to a wolf den, rendezvous, or kill site. To come upon a place where wolves had birthed new life, rallied with their pack, or gained sustenance from death would be an extraordinary and mystical experience. Of course our odds were slim, and it was important to simply embrace the journey.

One morning we walked into a dense forest of pine, hemlock, spruce, and fir without any wolf tracks to follow. I have no idea how cold it was, but I was bundled up and freezing, looking like a tourist in cumbersome bright-colored clothes. Insecure about my lack of experience and knowledge, I held back and observed the others, who were mostly confident and outgoing.

Some of the animals in the forest, for example martens and fishers, I had never even heard of. Worse than that, I was not able to visually identify a single track, whether I might know of the animal or not. Squirrel, hare, possum, and fox prints—they all looked the same to me.

When a guide named Liam noticed I was holding back, he pulled me aside to encourage my process. He told me how native clans tracked and hunted in groups like a wolf pack, using sensory perception and telepathy. He explained how he'd adopted their style, tracking in small groups with one person who forges ahead in fresh snow, looking for signs, while others follow by placing their feet in the same footsteps as their leader to conserve energy. He said it is common to follow a few animal tracks and then lose the trail. If that happens, one person knows to stay in the back and keep an eye on the last known imprint. When the leaders come to a dead end, one or two people will fan out, left and right, while the others stay centered. Most importantly, he assured me that every tracker has a unique skill that is valued and needed for the group to perform at its peak. Grateful for his perspective and wisdom, I relaxed and let go of the chatter in my mind to open my senses and receive information through acute sights, sounds, smells, touches, and intuitive hits.

On day three, we got lucky. One of the scouts found some fresh wolf tracks that stepped off of a fire lane and into the woods. As we moved into the dense forest and looked at the tracks before us, my heart did a flip. We saw by the shape of the tracks in the snow that a galloping lone wolf—we intuitively felt she was female—had raced up onto a ridge, possibly running for her life. Her power and speed were palpable as she threaded through tight tree trunks, weaving between and under snapped branches sticking out like sharp knives. Leaping five feet here and there over fallen logs, she had impressive precision. After the wolf came down off the ridge, we lost her trail and eventually gave up.

That night I barely slept. The moon was full, and I could not stop thinking about the lone she-wolf. Pondering and searching for the deeper meaning in her tracks, I thought of her as a kindred spirit. Although I did not have all the answers I wanted, I knew every wolf track I saw brought me one step closer to a wildness I was seeking.

On the fourth morning, we split into three groups so we could cover more ground. I ended up shoulder-to-shoulder with four guys in a beat-up little car. Noticing we were all wearing mukluks, we dubbed ourselves the Mukluk Gang. Liam was our guide, strong, gentle, and kind. Johnny was a soft-spoken young father who lived nearby. Chad, from Minneapolis, was a lot of fun and made enjoyable conversation. And then there was Gael. He was a young wildling covered in fur that he'd trapped, skinned, tanned, and tailored himself. His large furry *ushanka* hat was made out of beaver. His knee-length coat was coyote, and his mukluks were moose hide. He spoke in a heavy accent and appeared to perhaps be Russian. He carried a large mason jar full of rendered bear fat that he ate for nutrition and fuel and used to waterproof his mukluks.

While the other groups went off in different directions, we could not stop thinking about the lone wolf. Curious, we decided to go back and see if we could pick up her trail. Even though there were no visible tracks on the fire lane, we had a hunch that she may have crossed it. So we entered the woods on the other side, tracking in a line with a leader out in front. Ten minutes in, we heard a whoosh-ing sound in the air. Looking up we saw a large black raven with a piece of bright-red meat in his mouth. He was so close the flap of his wings stirred a light breeze on my face.

Eventually we found some wolf tracks that appeared to be in pursuit of a deer. When the trail disappeared, Johnny and Gael fanned out to see what they could find. As Gael took off to the left, I spontaneously followed him, placing my mukluks inside every deep hole his boots made in the snow. I wanted to walk in his footsteps at his pace and feel what it was like to be a wildling. He ran, veered, hopped, and twisted through the trees. I felt electric in my mirroring.

As Gael looped around to return to our base, he ran by a spruce tree and casually pointed down at a large shred of fresh deer hide. He kept going, but I stopped to inspect the white fur. As I touched the deerskin, it compelled me to stand up and turn around. When I did, my body went still. The silence was palpable. And then all of a sudden it registered.

As I looked through the trees before me, I saw in the distance a wide stretch of vibrant-red blood painted on snow. I gasped, and then I jumped up and down, screaming at the top of my lungs, "I found it! I found the kill site! Oh my god! I found the kill site!" I heard the guys laughing at my unusual reaction and remembered that trackers are normally quiet, communicating with sign language, bird calls, or animal sounds to minimize scaring the wildlife.

Standing on the edge of a portal where death begets life, I was silenced by the scene before me. The site told a beautiful, potent story, pulsing with red blood that symbolized both life and death. My heart raced as I felt in my viscera the brutal force that took the deer down. We saw marks in the snow where she was dragged, ripped apart, and devoured. And after a moment, I felt a warm sensation in my stomach as I imagined the wolf filling her empty belly with nourishing meat and the substance of bones.

Moving in closer, we inspected more details and were able to piece together more of the story. The wolf was indeed a female; we confirmed it with urine markings. On the other side of the site, we saw more wolf tracks racing in from different directions to assist with the kill. We saw marten, fisher, and fox tracks coming and going too and the wing tracks of a raven where he had lifted in flight from the snow.

By aging the tracks, we deduced the deer's life had been a three-day feast for a band of forest animals. Knowing the deer was a prey animal, I understood it was her higher purpose to serve as food for the wolves and others. In that way, the wolf and the deer had conspired to feed life on earth.

Nearby we found a rounded-out bed in the snow. The guys told me it's common for wolves to sleep near their kill. When I saw the circular imprint of the she-wolf's body, it tugged at my heartstrings to imagine her sleeping curled up in a ball with her tail covering her nose. I immediately laid myself down inside her frozen hollow and curled my body to fit. Curved in the wolf bed with my eyes closed, I felt the holy heartbeat of her wildness coursing through my veins.

Chapter Sixteen

matriarch elephant

A crone is a juicy older woman with zest, passions, and soul.
—*Jean Shinoda Bolen*

Matriarch Elephant is ancient, mammoth, strong, and wise. Highly respected and deeply loved, she is revered as the Grand Mother of all women and children in her herd. A compassionate and caring elder, she fosters connection, demonstrates integrity, and ushers her kin through life's cycles of joy and sorrow. Informed by experience, instincts, and the cellular memory of past lifetimes, Matriarch Elephant is the core and the glue of her clan.

During their seasonal migrations for food and water, the clan relies on their matriarch elephant to know in her bones when, where, and how they must go. Led by confidence and wisdom, the herd travels on circular routes through varied conditions of terrain and weather, averaging six miles or more per day. Traveling up and down, around, and about mountains, savannahs, deserts, and forests, they most often arrive at familiar places. But sometimes they are mysteriously lured by ancestral wisdom to areas that have not been seen by their clan for generations.

Enlivened by the wildness of wolf tracking and the study of native ancestral ways, I ardently and spontaneously said yes to more wild-woman adventures. Shortly after returning from Michigan, my new mentor, Robin Russell, told me about a two-week exploratory program he was leading in Africa. He described it as a cultural and wildlife immersion. Starting in the Kalahari Desert with the Dsùú Bushmen, participants would shadow the lifestyle of indigenous guides by observing and experiencing their intimate rapport with nature. Activities would include walking, wandering, playing, trapping, tracking, and foraging. Next the group would travel in open jeeps on a silent safari along the Khwai River in Botswana's Okavango Delta. The focus for this week would be communing with the animal kingdom through multisensory and telepathic communication. Deeply touched and compelled to go, I signed up on the spot without asking Rhys beforehand.

The trip to Africa was a bit more daring to tackle than my previous wild woman adventures. I had less than two months to prepare, and minimal details were made available up front. My euphoria subsided a bit when I received more information. It suddenly hit me that I would be gone for fifteen days in a foreign country that I had never visited before, and I did not have a buddy. Moreover, I read there would be no Internet or cell reception.

What I did know was to arrive at the airport in Maun, Botswana, on a specific date and to limit my bag's weight to twenty-six pounds, as we would be traveling to the Kalahari by a very small bush plane with load restrictions. Keeping it simple, I packed a duffle bag with one pair of pants, two pairs of shorts, one fleece, one rain jacket, four shirts, a pair of Keen hiking boots, socks, underwear, beanie, sun hat, toiletries, camera, binoculars, headlamp, journal, and pen.

Fueled by adrenaline on the day of my departure, I scrambled to get organized and out of the house on time. Driving to the airport with Rhys, I was excited to begin my adventure. It wasn't until we kissed good-bye at security that the enormity of my decision landed in the pit of my stomach like a rock. What was I thinking? I wanted to cry. My chest went tight. My heart felt gripped in a vise, making it hard to breathe. With every thump and throb, I felt a wave of pressure squeezing up and down my throat.

A gaggle of questions chased around in my mind. *What if something happens and I never see my family again? Will I be safe on my layover in Johannesburg? Who am I meeting in Maun? How will I find that person?* Most of all, I was thinking of snakes. What would I do if I encountered one?

Robin had left for Africa a week before me. Once there, he recorded a lesson and sent it to a moderator to share with his students. I was the only one in our group going to Africa, and I was terrified when I heard him describe a python outside his room.

Somewhere I read there are sixty species of snakes in Botswana and twelve are venomous. It's not that I was afraid of dying. It was the thought of a snake sneaking up on me that kept me on edge. I later realized that my heightened awareness of danger was actually good instincts kicking in. In Africa it's prudent to stay tuned into your surrounding environment with all of your senses. Your life depends on it.

Feeling anxious and nauseous when I finished with security, I picked up my phone, intending to call Rhys. I wanted him to save me, to come back and take me home. Instead I shook it off, and I walked to my gate. Once there I forced myself to sit down and observe my own my discomfort. I realized my body felt threatened and had kicked into fight-or-flight mode. Remembering the power of my breath, I deeply inhaled and exhaled. Finally, I was able to calmly assess all of my options and encourage myself to follow the path of mystery. Letting go, I leaned into my fears and boarded the plane.

Thirty-six hours later, I stepped onto the tarmac at the Maun international airport. It felt good to breathe in fresh air. Once inside the terminal, I saw a man holding up a sign with my name. He introduced himself as Mosi and said he worked at the place where our group was staying for one night. He offered to carry my small duffle bag as we walked outside and hopped into his truck.

Maun was a large rural town bustling with tourists, donkeys, pedestrians, bicycles, cars, and cows all vying for their place on the streets. Hence we moved slowly, giving me the chance to witness a hodgepodge of worlds. Once we made it through the urban conges-tion, the road opened up to a view of golden-white sand scattered with verdant shrubs and trees. Several locals were traveling by foot on the shoulder, and plenty of livestock wandered freely on and off the road.

Turning onto a side road, we drove past a few thatch-roofed shacks and cinder-block buildings before arriving at our lodge. Set near the Thamalakane River, the place was surrounded by marshy vegetation. As I stepped out of the vehicle, there was a hand-painted sign warning about the dangers of wildlife. I immediately imagined Cape buffalos, rhinos, and hippos whose size could overpower a human, as well as lions, hyenas, leopards, and crocodiles who would not hesitate to eat me for dinner! Then I thought of puff adders, black mambas, boomslangs, and cobras, so potent they could kill with me one strike!

Hearing Mosi call my name snapped me out of my trance, and I followed him through the gate into our complex and then along a curved path lined with round thatch-roofed bungalows. He opened the door to my room, and I followed him in. He handed me the key and offered to escort me to the courtyard, where my group was gathered for an orientation. There, I was warmly greeted by Robin and introduced to the other participants: a South African farmer, a photographer from Colorado, a naturalist from England, and a teacher from Findhorn in Scotland. Remarkably, there were also three leaders: Robin, a Bushmen friend/expert, and an animal communicator.

At nightfall we sat down at a long table in the courtyard under strands of small twinkling lights and feasted on a traditional African meal prepared by the lodge owners. *Seswaa*, a goat stew, was served to us over thick polenta with a leafy green side dish called *morogo*. After dinner we circled around a brilliant orange fire and bonded over stories of wild animals, totems, and our shared love of nature.

At the end of the night, I found myself warily walking alone as I returned by the long, dark path to my hut. I shivered to think of the python Robin had mentioned. Once inside my thatch-roofed bungalow, I was relieved to feel safe and sound, until I glanced up at the open space between the top of the walls and the roofline. Wondering what kind of insects and animals might visit my hut, I walked into the bathroom, where I was struck by the ominous sight of two enormous black spiders. Deciding not to shower, I headed straight for my bed. Quickly I inspected my sheets, turned off the lights, closed the mosquito net over my head, and lay down without changing my clothes.

All alone in the dark without cell service or Internet, I remembered reading somewhere that if I dug a tunnel from San Francisco straight through the center of the earth I'd eventually end up in Madagascar, which is not far from Botswana. Knowing I was literally halfway around the world, as far away as I could possibly get from my everyday life, I felt as if I had no husband, no children, no family, no friends, no dog, and no home. Lonely and scared, I curled myself into a ball and cried myself to sleep.

The next day after a grab-and-go breakfast, our group headed back to the airport to board the small bush plane that would take us to the western portion of the central Kalahari Desert for a week with the Dsùú Bushmen tribe. We flew low over vast forests, deserts, and grazing lands. The view was spectacular. An hour later, we landed on a private dirt airstrip located on a thirty-seven-thousand-acre wildlife reserve. A four-hour drive over rugged terrain to the nearest civilization, this place was truly wild and remote. My feet tingled when they touched ground on our motherland's soil. Suddenly I felt free.

Our home base for the next seven days and nights was a modest lodge located on a large piece of rare private property in the middle of the wildlife reserve. For three generations the owners had lived side by side with the Dsùú Bushmen, sharing their land. There were eight thatched chalets lined up in a row, each with a bed, a shower, and a couple of hours of solar-powered electricity at bedtime. There was also a common-area kitchen, a fire pit, and a covered outdoor dining table next to a large watering hole where zebras, kudus, gemsboks, elands, and ostriches came to loiter and drink in full view.

The owners also ran a ten-acre predator-conservation institute, situated behind the lodge, that housed wild dogs, leopards, and lions in large chain-link enclosures. The animals were rescued from the danger of being shot by livestock farmers for encroaching on their property. Our hosts said their ultimate goal was to relocate and return the animals to the wild, but they were having difficulty finding suitable habitat uncompromised by human development.

With a gentle warning, our hosts asked us to never go near the chain-link fences and to walk with a buddy back to our chalets at night. Furthermore, once inside our rooms, they advised us to stay there until morning. To emphasize caution, they told us about a lioness who often jumped the enclosure at night to go hunting. They said she always returned before daybreak.

That afternoon our group went into the bush and spread out, each of us relaxing in silence to practice absorbing wildlife sights, sounds, smells, patterns, and movements. Choosing an open space near scattered bushes and a manketti tree, I sat on the ground, closed my eyes, and took in several deep breaths. Noticing the tension in my body and the chatter in my mind, I imagined those barriers to connection releasing with every exhale.

Once softened, I partook in a sensual feast, replenishing myself with the beauty of nature. As the fragrance of sun-baked veld filled my lungs, the blue-green iridescence of Cape glossy starlings lit up my eyes. Stirring the air, white-backed vultures, bateleurs, and eagles spiraled above me while a medley of unknown insects made tiny tracks in the sand. Mesmerized by lingering trails and designs of activity, my heart skipped a beat as a shikra swooped in before me and swiftly snatched a sparrow midair. Perching on a branch with fresh food in her talons, I watched her hooked beak shred and consume the meal.

That night we sat around the campfire and learned more about the Dsùú Bushmen. As native hunter-gatherers who had lived in that region for twenty thousand years, they were one of the oldest surviving indigenous groups on earth, and they had been genetically identified as the source of all homo sapiens. My skin tingled to know I would soon meet the Bushmen, descendants of my original ancestors. I could hardly wait to learn more about their ancient ways of being.

My chalet was the last one on the end, just a stone's throw away from the lions. That night before I lay down, I opened the screened window above my bed so I could tune in to the night sounds of Africa. The lions were loudest, grunting in a guttural, continuous beat. I felt the pulse of their song all night long. The strength of their presence soothed me, and I thought of my father. He too was fierce and strong.

The next morning as we waited near the wild animals' watering hole, we watched a band of twenty or so Dsùú Bushmen approaching us. Moving slowly, they conserved energy for hunting and gathering, mimicking their animal brethren. The Dsùú were slender, with an average height of five feet. They had radiant smiles, golden-brown skin, and black nappy hair trimmed close to their heads.

Barefoot and mostly bare-skinned, the men were dressed in loin-cloths, each with a small kaross tied at their neck like a cape, readily available to carry things like firewood, food, or supplies. The women were dressed in hide slings as skirts. Each mother carried a baby on her back, using her kaross as a sling. The elder women wore theirs as halter tops.

I watched men, women, children, elders, and babies moving in sync as they approached. Their smiles, laughs, and touches were gentle toward each other, but the sum of their gathering was powerful. They radiated a collective glow that was different from the competitive groups I had experienced at home. Deeply touched by the tribe's cohesive, supportive, and expansive aura, I was able to experience their genuine love for each other from afar.

Once they arrived, the Dsùú stood before us with warm smiles as the translator introduced each of us. After exchanging greetings, my group began our week-long adventure of following the Dsùú into the bush. Through observation, interpretation, sign language, and trial and error, we learned how to identify medicinal plants, prepare and store water in ostrich eggs, and make snares with sticks and strings. We also tracked animals to learn their behaviors, and we foraged to gather morama beans and coffee bean seeds that we later roasted over a fire started by friction. All the while we sang songs, played games, laughed, and moved slowly, because the Bushmen place a high value on playing, resting, and mirth.

I was particularly attracted to the elder medicine man named Obiajulu, and I studied him intently. A thin, gentle man, he possessed the strength of a giant and the wisdom of Owl. Like most Bushmen, Obiajulu walked with a long, slender digging stick. On his shoulder, he carried a quiver full of arrows, a bow, and some tools. I was mesmerized by his eldership. When our group wandered the grasslands, I followed him closely, silently stepping in his tracks, imagining what it was like to be him.

I was not the only one in awe of Obiajulu. Everyone in our group was hoping to witness him perform a trance-dance healing according to his ancestral ways. Worried about my red cheek that was blistering in the African sun, and about two other women with health concerns, Robin asked Obiajulu if he would perform a healing ritual for the three of us. He replied yes.

On the night of our ceremony, we gathered in the bush under a vibrant full moon. Our group held back and respectfully watched as the Dsùú people conjured transformative energy to assist Obiajulu's trance. Clapping and chanting ancient medicine songs, the women sat in a circle, with the men at their center building a spirited fire. When the atmosphere was right, Obiajulu asked the three of us to join the circle.

Sitting with the women was intimate. Shoulder to shoulder and cross-legged knee to knee, we faced the howling fire with our root chakras grounded in the earth. The vibrations of their rhythmic song rippled up my spine. Amplifying the energy, Obiajulu and the men danced in a circle behind us, tapping, stomping, and thumping their feet hard into the ground. Intense, hot, and wild, the vortex of swirling vitality moved Obiajulu into an altered state. Trembling and shaking, he put his hand on my cheek and channeled energy down from the spiritual realm to assist with the healing of my feminine wound. I felt it that night. And for the next five months, my skin gradually cured from the inside out, accomplishing something no Western medicine had done and changing the face I showed to the world.

As if Obiajulu had magically conspired to further my remedy, the next day I would come face to face with a male lion. By happenstance our group crossed paths with the manager of the predator-conservation institute, and he offered to take us on a tour of the animal enclosures. Riding in an open-air safari jeep, we first visited a pack of African wild dogs. These canids are also referred to as "painted wolves" because they have unusual spotted fur of red, black, brown, white, and yellow. Their large round ears and social demeanor made them very sweet to observe.

Moving into the next enclosure, we pulled up to a lion named Simpson, who was sitting in tall grasses just five feet from where I sat at the end of our vehicle's bench. So close, his presence was palpable. I could almost reach out and touch his thick, glorious mane. When his luminous amber eyes locked into mine, I felt a power in my body that reflected both sides of the lion's nature. I sensed he was a virile beast, longing to devour blood, flesh, and bone, and yet I also saw him as a lionhearted sentient being. Once again, I thought of my father, who was manly like Simpson, and I acknowledged my gratitude for the ways he had enriched my life.

After our week with the Bushmen, we moved to the Okavango Delta and camped alongside a river in tents with a local safari guide named Alden. Most days and nights, we rode in safari vehicles searching for animals, focusing on our senses and keeping our talk to a minimum. One day we parked our jeep to go tracking and wandered through a graveyard of tree skeletons snapped off at the waist. The wispy shape of their trunks and branches looked like curling bare bones. Alden let us know we were walking through a forest of camel thorn trees that had been shaken, broken, and eaten by elands, giraffes, and elephants. He said it was nature's way of redesigning the land by causing death to create new life. Taking a closer look, we saw many green saplings and a variety of new plants emerging from the soil.

Meandering alone through the camel thorn woods, I found a very large bone, more than three feet long and most likely an elephant femur. Squealing with joy, I picked up the heavy bone with two hands for inspection and then pushed it above my head. It was the largest bone I'd ever come across in all of my collecting.

Suddenly compelled to walk a few feet in another direction, I stumbled upon an enormous elephant skull that was rolled back, facing the sky. The moment I saw her, an invisible force touched my skin and swept through my body. This was sacred space. Feeling the animal's spirit profoundly, I was moved to tears. Sensing the bone was ancient, soothing, and wise, I knelt down and laid my face upon hers.

When Alden caught up to me, he told me the story of a matriarch elephant named Ele. He said day after day, for over sixty-five years, this majestic elder had led her large family of females and children to food and water using routes that were genetically etched in her memory from previous lifetimes.

Alden said that on many occasions he watched Ele and her clan walk to a nearby watering hole along the worn path near my feet. But one day, Ele never made it to the water. Halfway there, she collapsed to her knees and took her last breath in that position. In that way, she was preserved for quite some time because the large predators could not get to her underbelly. Eventually, her body was transformed, and all that remained were her bones, symbolizing her eternal spirit, that part of her which can never die.

He told me that her family still stops to visit their beloved elder each time they take this path to the watering hole. Touching her bones with their trunks, they pause with great emotion and offer low rumbling sounds. Alden said it's clear they miss her graceful, strong, and wise presence and deeply mourn their loss.

Resting my head on Ele's skull, I thought of her as an inspiration and role model for my eldership years. Reflecting on the past two weeks, I saw my time in Africa as a journey of profound transformation, guiding me further on my path from motherhood to a wise-woman phase. By following the tracks, symbols, and signs, I was led to the motherland to be shaken open and tuned to the bone.

Chapter Seventeen

black panther

I am Woman. Let me do what I do.

—*Pixie Lighthorse*

Black Panther is a feminine creature. She is slinky, sexy, and sensual, sauntering her way through the jungle. Frequently resting and sleeping, she also sprints in small bursts with great speed. Swift on her feet, she can scale tall trees, balance on branches, and leap to seize prey in midair. Curious, independent, and spontaneous, Black Panther has a mind of her own. This wild feline does what she wants to do and goes where she wants to go.

Black Panther is a totem of darkness. She is mysterious, graceful, and aware, hunting on a moonless night. A solitary creature, she glides through the shadows, silently stalking her mark. Stealthy and fierce with powerful jaws, she crushes her meal, transforming death into fuel for her life. A potent dark goddess who walks between worlds, Black Panther is also a bridge. Half material, half ethereal, she can see without eyes. She knows who you are to the bone.

In Africa I was energized and initiated, but I did not know how to integrate the experience with my daily life. Tired of managing two estates and multiple identities, I desperately wanted to simplify by selling our Atherton house and moving to the ranch full-time. My family did not concur.

Location was key. Rhys and the kids considered Portola Valley a long way from civilization and more suitable as a vacation spot than a home. They loved living in Atherton, near the hustle and bustle of friends, restaurants, stores, and jobs. Every morning Rhys worked out with his buddies at our country club down the street and hobnobbed at the local coffee shop before heading out to work with various close-by companies.

Sentimental value was also at stake. Ella and Jake implored me not to abandon the home that had nurtured them for nearly two decades. It was their sanctuary and playground and a place where their friends loved to gather. Rhys was also very attached to the Atherton estate. It was his dream home and a symbol of hard-earned success.

The last factor was time and money. The ranch house would require a sizable addition if we wanted to consolidate our two properties. For many reasons, moving to the ranch seemed impossible, so I limped along with the status quo.

Sixteen months after my trip to Africa, Jake left for his freshman year in college. That is when Hawk first visited me in Atherton. Following his advice, I drove to the ranch for some spiritual sustenance, but it was only a temporary reprieve. More depleted than ever and grieving the end of an era, I fell sick into bed for one month with the flu and a recurring sinus infection. Numb from the magnitude of life, duties, and expectations, I had no idea what to do next. With my stepson's three children nearby and more on the way, I could have easily stepped into the role of a babysitting grandmother, but something inside me was demanding a change. I had been studying, working, and fighting my way toward it. On the verge, I could not give up now.

Then one night Black Panther appeared in the landscape of my dreams. Floating above the scene, I had an aerial view of the huntress. She was prowling at dusk on the fringe of a suburb that looked like a giant square maze shaped out of tall, manicured box hedges. I perceived the town to be Atherton and recognized my house at the center. Silently sleuthing and sensing, she circled the puzzle three times, carefully choosing an entrance. Crossing into my precinct with her front-left paw, the big cat awoke me with a start. Sitting upright in bed, wide-eyed and breathless from the touch of a dark feline predator, my heart pulsed to the beat of an African drum.

In that ethereal dream I was both the hunter and the hunted. Upon waking I reflected on my life and where it was headed. I wanted to become a spiritual elder, but I did not know how to walk my talk. Symbolically lost in suburbia, I had no idea how to get out. Black Panther was a clue. Her wildness was moving me.

Standing in my power, I pleaded with Rhys to consider the move. After a lot of serious discussion, he finally relented, and we met with our architects to initiate the design of an addition to the ranch house. Ecstatic, I immersed myself in the eighteen-month process and began spending more time in Portola Valley, managing the construction, connecting with nature, and envisioning the final phase of my life.

Then, four months before our move-in date, my sister Kelly sent me a video of an adorable stray cat bopping along at her feet making all sorts of cute "look at me" noises. The tortoise-shell-colored feline had been hanging around her cul-de-sac for the past week. Kelly and her neighbors had fallen head over heels in love with the alluring little feline, but their pets were getting territorial. One of the elder cats in particular was very upset about the interloper, so the owner let everyone know she would be taking the stray to the pound soon. Worried, Kelly posted "Found Cat" signs all over town.

I was not a cat person, nor did I want a new pet, but something about this feline with glowing eyes the color of a harvest moon stirred my soul and called to me. It seemed like she was part canine too, with her cheerful personality and her habit of following strangers while meowing at their feet. There was one more thing about her that caught my eye. She glistened like gold. Her short dark fur was dappled with gilt in special places like her chest, where brilliant flecks of gold poured down to her front leg and pooled at the bottom to highlight a magic golden paw. This feline and her left foot beckoned my heart like an open door to an ancient Egyptian temple. I could not resist her. But what was I thinking? My primary totem was Wolf. My character was alpha. My family was a pack. My best friend was my dog. I was canine for life—or so I thought.

My relationship with Marga ran deep. She was the most beautiful dog I had ever seen, with deep tropical-ocean-blue eyes and long, soft fur colored with marbles of gray, blue, white, black, and chestnut. People referred to her as a Velcro dog because she rarely left my side when I was home, and she was not interested in other people. I knew Marga would be heartbroken to share my attention. Plus, she had already proven to the neighborhood that she would not tolerate cats in her vicinity.

There was also the matter of Rhys, who hadn't wanted a single dog, let alone two pets. He was in Europe at the time, and he happened to call me right after I saw the video. Dropping a bomb, I announced, "I found a cat I want to adopt."

"What? Absolutely not," he replied. "Why do you want a cat? Marga will go crazy."

I changed the subject, but he knew I was serious, and he worried the whole way home. Logically, I knew Rhys was right. We were just starting to savor more personal freedom as empty nesters. Another pet was another being to care for.

My mind went into overdrive: *What if the cat claws our furniture? What if she runs away? If I leave to rescue her, who will take care of Marga while Rhys is away? Kelly lived five hundred miles away. How could I possibly squeeze this into my overbooked schedule? But if I could make it happen, should I buy a five-hundred-dollar plane ticket, or drive sixteen hours round-trip?* It was a lot to consider in twenty-four hours, but time was running out for this cat.

Acting on impulse birthed from my heart, I called Kelly the next morning to say, "I want the cat!"

"*What?*" She was shocked. This was the last thing she expected, because I lived so far away.

Kelly immediately told her next-door neighbor I was going to adopt the cat, but the lady would not wait for me to get there. Instead she took the little cat to the pound. When I heard that, I fell to the floor sobbing.

Tracking down the cat after that took time and determination. The Humane Society was massive, with multiple campuses and an automated phone system. After navigating a series of messages and options, Kelly would be put on hold, and after one hour of waiting her call would drop. It went on like that for twenty-four hours.

The next day, Kelly finally got through and learned the cat was on hold for exactly seventy-two hours after she was turned in, as a courtesy to see if her owner would claim her. The hold would end at noon on Friday. If still unclaimed, the cat would be slated for public adoption. At that point, she would be in a black hole until Saturday morning at nine, when the facility opened its doors to the public for a mass meet-greet-and-adopt event — first come, first served.

Kelly and I feared someone else might snatch our kitten up. We schemed how to be first in line for adoption on Saturday and wondered how early people lined up. Then we discovered that I was not eligible to adopt since I was from out of the area. To make it even more complicated, we learned that once someone formally adopts a pet and pays the fees, it's mandatory for the shelter to keep the cat to spay her, so she would not be available for pickup until Monday.

With a lot of juggling, Kelly had cleared her schedule so she could adopt the cat for me on Saturday, but she would not be able to pick her up on Monday because she was headed out of town on Sunday morning. We were in a real pickle. The emotional experience was harrowing as we agonized about how to rescue the cat in a cage.

On Thursday afternoon, in a flash of inspiration, I told Kelly to call the shelter and claim the cat as her lost pet. Why not? She had photos and a description to back it up. But time was running out, and we had less than twenty-four hours before she would be irretrievable. The next morning, I hopped on a six a.m. flight and then took a cab forty miles north. Kelly and I met at the shelter exactly three hours before the deadline.

Sitting in the parking lot, we were scared. We felt guilty for lying. What if they could tell the cat did not belong to Kelly? What if they wouldn't give her to us? For thirty minutes, we reviewed Kelly's story to get the plausible details straight. Once the doors opened, we went to the counter and claimed her.

When Kelly identified the cat, they put her in a carrier and escorted us to the front desk, but we weren't in the clear yet. There were hard questions to be answered: *How old is she? Why didn't you spay her?*

Did you know she has ear mites, which are typical for a street cat but not for a house pet?

Flustered but quick on her feet, Kelly answered, "She's around a year old. We didn't spay her because we didn't have time." And sheepishly she threw in, "I did not know she had ear mites."

The lady hesitated, gave us a suspicious look, and then handed us the bill. Once Kelly paid up, we ran to the car as fast as we could. Next it was back to the airport, where I boarded the plane and set my new cat in her carrier under the seat for takeoff. During the flight I pulled her bed chamber up onto my lap, where she lay full of grace — no rustles, no peeps.

After a weeklong journey of conniving and fetching my feline, I yearned to be still and experience her essence. But as we walked across the threshold, chaos was quick to greet us. Marga smelled cat. She paced the room. Wheezing and drooling, she searched for the intruder. Then her soulful blue eyes locked onto mine, piercing me with her pain. Her look said, "How could you?"

I had to decide right away how to keep the cat safe. It wasn't ideal to have her in a separate building, but I figured the pool house was the only way to shield her from the dog. I left Marga in the main house and carried the cat outside.

The pool house was fit for a queen. It included a spacious living room, bedroom, bathroom, and kitchen with an entire wall of French doors that opened to a lush, colorful garden full of birds, majestic trees, and water. A vigorous pond teemed with wildlife, cattails, and water lilies near a saltwater swimming pool that glistened like an aqua-colored ocean at sunset.

Once she was safely settled with food and water, it was time to play. I grabbed a long, stretchy strap from a bikini top that was hanging on a doorknob, and I wiggled it across the floor like a snake. My new cat quickened like a panther, tracking her prey with unrelenting focus and stealth. Hiding and pouncing, she nailed her target every time, no matter how quickly I snapped the cord or how fast I ran from room to room. The strap served as a conduit, enlivening us by sending energy between her end and mine. Our connection deepened on multiple layers: physically through the string, mentally through the game, and emotionally through a mutual thrill of the chase.

In addition to her wild nature, there was something profound and mysterious about this cat. Her postures and poses were regal. She had the air of a black panther with venerable eyes. In a flash, I knew her name was Cleopatra. She was "Her Majesty," with the aura of an ancient queen.

Every day I told Marga that my love for her would never diminish and that Cleopatra needed a home. I begged her to be friends with the cat. As I implored her, I imagined all three of us cuddling on the couch together, hoping she would like my vision. Marga's stressed-out attitude and lack of cooperation was her answer.

The only option I had was to split the estate and my time between dog and cat. Luckily, our two-acre property was already fenced around the perimeter and sectioned in between. We confined Marga to the main house and front yard. Cleopatra had the pool house in the back. Symbolically, my pets were reflecting the dichotomies that had exhausted and plagued me. Marga represented my exterior life, my public persona, while Cleopatra reflected my hidden inner world.

Cleopatra's abode doubled as my spiritual studio. When I worked there I absorbed her and she absorbed me. There was a healing power in the silence of her presence. Her feline ways softened my dominant canine character. Under her influence I naturally opened and received bits of inspiration, ideas, and messages that randomly floated into my mind. It seemed she was my muse.

Cleopatra was also acutely tuned in to my spiritual work. There were beautiful altars sprinkled throughout the pool house on side tables, counters, and consoles. Crystals and gemstones of lapis lazuli, malachite, and onyx; amulets; candles; and flowers were arranged in patterns of sacred geometry to radiate my prayers and good intentions. Quite often Cleopatra would surprise me by placing her sovereign self in the middle of a shrine. It took my breath away to look up and behold the exquisite symmetry she created with the placement of her pose. She was majestic in the midst of colorful cloths, magic wands, towering crystals, and all sorts of other talismans.

I did not like leaving Cleopatra in the pool house by herself at night, so after a month I brought her into the main house. Marga suffered from severe arthritis and could not climb stairs. Cleopatra figured out Marga's limitations and navigated the house and the dog with stealth. Upstairs was Cleopatra's realm, and downstairs belonged to Marga. Most of the time, Cleopatra relaxed on the upper landing, enjoying us from a distance. When Marga noticed, she barked till our ears hurt. Unflustered, Cleopatra lounged like a panther on a tree branch, dangling her limbs between the banister posts.

The animals reflected how I was evolving. My two worlds were still split, but they were coming closer together. Marga was held down at ground level, symbolizing my domesticated nature, while Cleopatra was upstairs, representing my higher self (my soul) as a creative and untamable creature.

During the day, I started taking Cleopatra into the backyard. She never ran away and always came in when I called. One afternoon, Marga found a way into the backyard where Cleopatra and I were sunning. With an explosion of determination and fury, Marga chased Cleopatra to the fence. Faster than a bullet, Cleo shot to the other side and beyond. Shaking and distraught, I felt a pit open in my stomach. I took Marga into the house and called for Cleopatra, but she did not respond.

That night under the moon, I howled Cleopatra's name over and over and over. I finally gave up at three a.m. and closed the doors to keep out the rats. Heartsick, I climbed into bed between Marga and Rhys.

The next afternoon while I was gone, Rhys—who had once been angry that I had adopted the cat—roamed our backyard calling, "Here, kitty, kitty, kitty." She appeared, but just as he was about to pick her up, he saw a very large black cat approaching. Rhys told me that when Cleopatra turned her head and saw the interloper, she took off like a bat out of hell and both cats scaled the fence. According to Rhys, it was the biggest damn cat he'd ever seen, and Cleopatra was scared as hell.

Once again I howled with doors wide open. Lo and behold, she finally came in at three a.m. The first thing I did was sit down on the floor. Purring and rubbing, she marked my skin with the scent of her fur. I was so grateful to have her back home. Never again did we see the mysterious black tomcat. I could not help but wonder if he was a spirit in disguise sent to us for some one-time magic.

When I first adopted Cleopatra, there was a lot of confusion among three different vets as to whether or not she was neutered. I did not want to traumatize her with surgery she may have already endured, so I had planned to keep her inside, or outside with me, through the spring. If she went into heat, I would spay her. She never showed signs of estrus, but after her night out I did wonder what might have transpired between her and the black cat.

My wonder turned to worry when I had a strong premonition that Cleopatra was indeed pregnant. I could barely handle one cat and one dog, let alone kittens. And we were moving in two months. At that time, I was studying with a mystical teacher named Dara. Rattling off my fears to her, I complained: Raising kittens is work and I don't have the time. They will destroy our new home. There are too many cats in the world. I'll never be able to give the kittens away.

When I finished, Dara shut me down. She said it was a waste of my time and emotion to worry. I had no proof, and the odds were slim this early in the year. All of a sudden, I felt stupid for imagining that Cleopatra was pregnant.

A month later when I discovered tapeworm segments on Cleopatra's bed, I called my vet. The receptionist said the doctor's schedule was full, but I could pick up some pills and give them to Cleopatra at home. My instincts kicked in once again, and I said, "I think my cat might be pregnant. If so, are the pills safe?"

There was a long pause before she replied, "I'll have to check. Please hold." I imagined she was thinking I was irresponsible if my cat was pregnant and she was annoyed that I wasn't even sure. As I waited, I felt guilty making her research alternative meds on such a busy day.

Finally she told me there was an injection for tapeworm that was approved for pregnant cats, but of course I would have to bring her in for that. They were swamped, but she promised to squeeze us in. When I arrived, a young vet tech came out to the lobby to get Cleopatra. She asked me to stay there while she administered the shot in the back. The waiting area was full, and the technician was in a hurry. It didn't matter. I blurted out for all to hear, "I think my cat is pregnant. Will you check her nipples to see if you agree?"

Puzzled or irked, she scrunched her forehead and rolled her eyes, "Uh, sure."

I sat down and never looked up. I was embarrassed to meet eyes with anyone in the room. When the technician returned with Cleopatra, she announced, loud enough for all to hear, "We gave her the shot and then we looked her over. She shows no signs of being pregnant."

"Thank you," I said, and I hurried out the door with the cat under my arm and my tail between my legs.

Yet I felt Cleopatra was transforming. Was it intuition or fear? The changes were subtle but familiar to me: her walk was slightly different, she ate a tad more food, and she asked for more affection. The most auspicious sign was my hand, which dipped like a dowsing rod to water when my arm hovered near her womb. I felt our intimacy was growing deeper, as if we were pregnant as one.

It wasn't long after that when I noticed traces of blood in Cleopatra's urine. I scheduled a visit with my vet, but this time I kept quiet about the imagined pregnancy. It felt like revealing devil worship to speak of my extrasensory perceptions. Without tangible proof, the people I had shared my thoughts with did not have respect for my intuition on this matter. Doubting had subdued my voice.

After some pleasantries and a weigh-in, Dr. Ross said to his assistant, "I need a urine sample. While she's standing, hold her tail up with a cup underneath it." Quickly, before I realized what he was going to do, Dr. Ross grabbed Cleopatra's tummy and squeezed it tight. A horrific shriek arched out of Cleopatra. The force of it threw my body back as it pierced my ears, stabbed my heart, and rattled my innards. Wide-eyed and spooked, Dr. Ross froze in shock. Snapping out of it, he took the cup from his tech. With a puzzled face he said, "That's not urine; it's clear."

I cried out to him, "I think she might be pregnant!"

Dr. Ross's face went gray. "I must have squeezed her womb. This might be amniotic fluid. If so, I may have killed her kittens." My knees went weak, and I nearly fainted for Cleopatra. With much urgency, Dr. Ross exclaimed, "We need to do a sonogram right now to see if she's pregnant." He invited me to follow him as he rushed, with her in his arms, out the door and through the operating room. All heads went up and eyes were on us as we flew by a dog, splayed out and open midsurgery.

In a back room full of medical equipment, I felt scared and sick to my stomach to witness the grave consequences of silencing my intuition. As Cleopatra lay calmly on the table without a fuss, they gooped her up and waved the sonogram wand all over her belly. Soon, with a ton of relief and excitement, Dr. Ross showed me the flashes of light and said, "Yes, she is pregnant! I see four beating hearts!"

The energy shifted and it felt surreal. The jolt from Cleopatra's trauma had cracked the stiffness of routine wide open, allowing places for light to seep in. Warm energy swirled around us as we connected over common purpose. A larger crowd began to gather as the allure of new life infused everyone with an alternative form of medicine.

The queen and I stayed there for twenty minutes with five doctors and nurses in a womb of warm energy. At the center of our circle, Cleopatra was stretched out in repose, calm, cool, and collected like Black Panther.

In a narrow-minded Silicon Valley that served the affluent and highly educated, Cleopatra was a goddess. Her mysteriously feminine ways were wild and spontaneous. She harkened us back to the old days when people respected animals as medicine, teachers, and guides.

Our move date was drawing nearer. Several weeks earlier, I had started working full-time with a team of four professional organizers. Grace, the leader, had estimated it would take us nearly three months to sort and pack eleven thousand square feet of stuff my family had accumulated over eighteen years. In addition, we were challenged to reduce our possessions by 55 percent, as the new ranch house would be much smaller than our Atherton home. The magnitude of our mission was daunting, and the process became a heavy, piercing ballad to my chapters as mother and wife.

Everything in my life had meaning. It was important for me to methodically see, touch, and reflect on every single item at our Atherton estate, from clothing to papers to toys, dishes, books, heirlooms, tchotchkes, and junk. With each piece came a memory and significance that touched my heart in deep places. Every large and tiny object caused me to awaken and relive an aspect of myself, after which I had to decide if I would keep, donate, or trash it.

Mothering teenagers was so exhausting that I had forgotten the wonder years of Ella and Jake's childhoods. In fact, there were periods of time when I doubted I had been an adequate mother. But my mind shifted and my body softened as I burrowed into Ella's drawers and discovered her treasures from Camp Finbarr and jerseys from soccer. There were dolls that I had given her for Christmas and little love notes from her friends. Tiny tap shoes, ballet shoes, and tutus tugged at my heartstrings and flooded my face with tears. I remembered how much I loved being a mother and the good times we had when Lela was there to support me.

Stilled by my reverie, I laid my body on Ella's white downy bed to smell her soft pillows and further soak in her essence. Scanning the room from that view, I saw her stuffed animals piled high on a couch and her trophies lined up on a shelf. There were posters of her football idol, John Terry; photo collages of her laughing and hugging with friends; and a necklace of her pacifiers I had strung on a string like a lei.

Jake's room had the same nostalgia, except its fragrance was of dirty socks. In his drawers I found Pokémon cards, Pikachu figurines, and Ash getups with props. His chairs were piled high with junk, and his desktop was sprinkled with eraser crumbs. Half of his posters were drooping, and his lamps were broken from ball hits.

Grace was hardworking, compassionate, and protective of me as I endured and grieved the transition. She patiently listened when I complained, and she gave me hugs like a mother when I cried. She lifted me up with her grace in a thousand different ways by consistently smiling and lightening my load. Our relationship was intimate and sacred. I trusted her in my home with my family and my things.

Monday through Friday, Grace and her circle of women helpers came to manage the piles I sorted in advance for them. They drove carloads of donations to various sites, took garbage to the dump, and carefully packed everything I wanted to keep. Extremely organized, Grace prepared an inventory list for every box that outlined the contents and told which room it came from and which room it was to go to in the new house.

The last month of packing and moving was brutal. My emotions ran like a roller coaster to great heights of euphoria from hard-earned progress followed by stomach-turning drops each time I discovered another hidden cupboard or closet full of goods. Eventually I ran out of energy, and my spirit lay flat on a platform. Coming so far for so long and still seeing only mountains before me made it seem like I had an impossible truth to conquer.

Nearing the end, I was a haggard zombie, disoriented inside a gray mansion that echoed loneliness from its empty walls. Cardboard boxes, dust bunnies, and cobwebs were my only decor. I was homeless, living in a house that was not a home, and I was lost without sight of myself. I'd stripped myself down to the bone—again—in order to rebuild myself from that point. All my beautiful facades and fronts were gone. The walls of my mansion—behind which I stood—and my expensive zip code were disappearing. My life was in a phase of decay and death.

Two weeks before our move-in date, I was asked to stay away from the ranch house. A team of people were going to finalize our home so it would be organized, cozy, and decorated on our first night, a sharp contrast to our last move. I was so grateful I cried.

One afternoon in the midst of their process, I had to break the rules and go to the ranch house for a meeting with the painters. When I walked in unannounced, the feeling and the sight took my breath away and lifted my heart to my throat. I stood still and in awe, observing four organizers, three decorators, five movers, and a myriad of craftsmen humming in sync.

There was a rhythm and a balance in the hustle and bustle of a perfectly orchestrated cosmos. Grace stood on a ladder in the kitchen unpacking and organizing dishes. Fazzio was hemming handmade curtains on rods while Donna was steaming the wrinkles. Jerry, the foreman, was walking with the plumber as two movers slipped by them, unfazed, with a couch. Every room was jam-packed with furniture, papers, boxes, people, and stuff. Every person was tapped into the flow.

The house was radiant and glowing with exquisite design, colors, woodwork, and artistry. I squealed with delight and marveled out loud at each person's talent. Gushing, I couldn't thank them enough. Everyone was smiling and happy to be part of the dream team. They loved their work and were uplifted to be valued.

Finally I spent my first night in our new house. The kids were away at college and Rhys out of town, so it was just Marga, Cleopatra, and me. With the windows wide open and my lungs full of fresh air, I was lulled into deep slumber by a hymn of hooting owls and yipping coyotes.

The next morning at sunrise I sat on our deck facing the Santa Cruz Mountains. They radiated a giant, green, and glorious peace that moved through my heart and every cell of my body. As my chest expanded with life-force and my ears tickled with birdsongs, my eyes watered and my body heaved. I wept with humility and gratitude for the magnificent grace that was present. And I marveled at the forces guiding me home to sacred places inside and outside of myself. I had moved through a process of death that had birthed a phase of new life.

Cleopatra taught me how to trust my intuition and access my feminine ways. Her large presence in my life was ushering me through the shift from earthly Wolf Mother to spiritual Feline Elder. Cleopatra the cat, half tame and half wild, was my bridge to Black Panther totem.

Chapter Eighteen

skunk

It's not about the wound. It's about where the wound leads you.

—David Pond

Skunk is a beautiful creature, lavishly covered in sensual fur. Jet black and pure white, her coloring illustrates duality. Through nighttime, daytime, dark aspects and light, she restores what is contrary with balance. Confident, fearless, independent, and calm, her keynote is respect; she owns it. Content with herself, Skunk is original, peaceful, and strong. Her easygoing presence is alluring to many, but there are some who mistake her manners.

Skunk is often a solitary creature who values being alone and will spray those who don't heed her cautions. Firmly but gently, she will offer three levels of warning to any being who blocks her flow or threatens her safety. First she will send a message to back off by raising her tail like a flag and stamping her feet on the ground. If the menace persists, she will dance to a rhythm of charge, stomp, pull back, charge, stomp, pull back. Only if the danger remains will Skunk twist her body into the shape of a *U* and aim her rear end's spray nozzle into the face of her foe. As a last resort, she will send a burning musk into the offender's eyes. Pungent, spicy, sexy, and steamy, the heavy scent will linger. Although some may think it foul, Skunk's perfume has the power to awaken dormant ribbons of life-force.

When we sold our Atherton home and moved to the ranch, I was fifty-five years old. Looking back, it was clear to me that everything I had endured and experienced over a period of five and a half decades was an opportunity to further define who I was on the inside. By fully immersing myself into my heartaches and feeling them deeply, I came to know myself better. What I found were parts of my original self that had been tamed, suppressed, or hidden. Consciously aging and striving to stand in my power as a spiritual feminine elder, I prayed I was near ready to share the wisdom of my discoveries with those who were searching for deeper meaning in their lives.

As if to affirm my intention, a young mother friend of mine named Shannon unexpectedly invited me to her home for a croning ceremony in my honor.

Harkening back to an ancient feminine tradition, she wanted to celebrate my passage from Mother to Wise Woman Crone and my transition from Atherton to Portola Valley. Astonished, I felt a huge swell of warm energy lift and expand my heart. I sat there in a moment of silence before I gratefully accepted her invitation.

Just a few days later when I arrived at Shannon's home, her two young daughters, Stella, age seven, and Esther, age three, greeted me gaily at their front door. Jumping, squealing, and smiling from ear to ear, each girl took one of my hands. They whisked me through their house and out the back door into a garden of sensory delight.

A festival of large and small plants lured me into their kingdom. Enchanted by their welcome and gracious hospitality, I dove in with all of my senses. Following the song of a red-breasted house finch, I beheld pink and white peonies, merry yellow daffodils, climbing red roses, and delicate cream-colored sweet peas. When I walked around the garden to a raised bed of greenery, Shannon invited me to sample a potpourri of vegetables and herbs. Touching the mint, lavender, and lemon balm left the scent of their oils on my fingertips. A sprig of parsley on my tongue cleansed my palate.

Relaxed and ready, Shannon motioned for me to sit down on a wooden chair near some sweet-smelling freesias. A few moments later, she and her two daughters stood before me, holding a wreath in their hands. Gazing up, Shannon declared to the sky, "This wise woman's name is Lucinda. We the maidens and a mother bestow our blessings upon this crone with a crown that we have made from this magical garden."

Placing the garland on my head, she continued, "May the rosemary offer you protection going forward and remembrance of all that has passed, and may the salmon-colored zinnia infuse you with spiritual endurance." When I stood up, we held hands in a circle and quietly absorbed the divine nature of our setting and my juncture.

Crowned and barefoot, wearing a long flowing dress, I followed the girls through a gate and stepped onto a trail that headed uphill through a mountain forest. At that moment, a gray-striped cat appeared and joined our procession. Strolling, turning, and twisting, we ascended on a meandering trail lined with manzanita, toyon, and oak.

At the top of a ridge, we met up with Shannon's friends who had just moved here from Brazil: Maria, the mother; Luana, her seven-year-old daughter; Yuri, her four-year-old son; and Camilla, their Siamese cat. Right on cue, the striped-gray feline presented us to the blue-eyed chocolate-point cat with a resounding meow and then turned around to head back down the hill.

Followed by one cat, one boy, two women, and three girls, I, as a consecrated elder, entered a mystical, magical redwood forest. As I stepped onto the thick spongy duff, I felt a shift in the energy and looked up to see dozens of giant furry-barked tree people gathering around us with open, leaf-laden arms.

Inside the harbor of their sanctum all of us were free to be child-like. Giggling, frolicking, and playing, we admired found treasures, befriended the fairy folk, shared fanciful stories, and wielded scepters made from long sticks. As daylight turned to twilight, our merriment came to an end, and we bid farewell to all of our friends.

Back at their home, I embraced Shannon, Stella, and Esther heart to heart and thanked them for seeing me as an elder. Our ceremony served to anchor my ethereal vision of eldership into my physical body. They ushered me through an important rite of passage that helped me synthesize my spiritual and human nature.

The next morning, Marga was not well. At thirteen, her breathing was shallow and she suffered from arthritis. The stress of our move had exacerbated her ailing and discomfort. At first she was wheezing, and then her weak back legs gave out. When she fell to the ground, I felt a stab in my heart. Knowing it was time to let her go, I called the vet and asked him to come to our house.

For her final hour, I cuddled with Marga on my bedroom floor, recalling all the ways that the meaning of her name rang true. She was indeed the animal path that I followed to my innermost heart. A domesticated Wolf, Marga had truly been my best friend, mirror, and guide for more than a decade.

When the doctor arrived, Rhys, Marga, and I walked with him out to an oak grove on the edge of the property, where Chase had dug a six-foot-deep hole, hitting water near the bottom. The vet gave Marga a sedative to relax her, and she gracefully lay down near the mouth of her grave. Holding her head in my hands for a while, I said my last words while the others stood watch behind me. When Marga and I were ready, I laid myself down on the grass beside her, eye to eye, nose to nose, and mouth to mouth. When I nodded to the vet, he gave her the lethal injection then quickly stepped back, honoring our holy space.

Gazing into Marga's ocean-blue eyes, I could feel her slight breath on my face. It startled me when she sucked in and released a quick wind. For a second, I thought she was gone, but then quickly she drew in and out two more times. On her third and last out breath, a force pushed my head back, causing me to suck in air. Feeling a warm swipe on my heart, I sensed her soul was leaving a trace before it traveled through a portal to heaven. Knowing she was gone, I buried my face in her fur, and I cried. When I was done, Rhys and I lowered her with rope on a fabric stretcher down into earth's watery tomb.

Animals have taught me there is movement in death as it clears space for something new to enter. Marga's transition guided me to move and grow. I would always be Wolf, but Cleopatra had much to teach me about her feminine feline ways.

Cleopatra was due any day, and I began to prepare a sacred place for her to birth her kittens. Our basement bathroom at the end of a long hallway was perfect. It had heated tile floors and a cozy built-in wooden bench with enough room for me to sit between two different whelping boxes. Both were made out of cardboard and soft towels.

One box was square and upright with four sides. The other was taller and lay on its side. I didn't know if the queen would prefer to hop into a contained chamber or crawl into a tunnel that opened with a view, so I left both birthing beds set up and Cleopatra visited them often.

Seven nights after Marga's crossing, I suspected Cleopatra was going into labor, because she was unusually affectionate with me in bed. Burying the curve of her spine under the covers and pressing it firmly into my belly, she wanted to meld into me. As we spooned, she wiggled and writhed. Not wanting to disturb her natural process, I was fine if she happened to birth her babies right there.

But at three a.m., Rhys woke up and shrieked, "That cat is going to have her babies in our bed. Take her downstairs!" With that, Cleopatra jumped in the air, and I huffed my way out of the room. I hurried down the stairs and hallway to her room as Cleopatra followed at my feet the whole way. When I sat on the bench in between the two boxes, she crawled into the one turned on its side. After a few minutes, I was thirsty. When I hurried upstairs for some water, Cleopatra gave me the dickens, howling and nipping at my heels. She was mad that I had left and demanded I return to the birthing room right away.

One hour later, as Cleopatra lay on her side in the den, I intuited that she wanted me to place my left palm on her belly. When I did, her womb contracted and moved my hand like a wave. Lifting her head, she let out a meow, and her first baby slipped out. With great instinct, Cleopatra immediately began licking the gooey, moist sac tinged with blood to clean and stimulate her newborn until it transformed into a fluffy whimpering kitten. Three more times my hand connected with the point of creation where a new soul enters the earth plane to start a new life. With each birth, I felt a rush of energy that echoed from Cleopatra's womb up through my arm to my heart.

For the next eight weeks, I lived in a warm, dark den with five cats, three tortoise-colored and two black. Holding, sensing, and observing, I was in awe to witness every second of their development. I tracked their progress hour by hour, expanding their horizons when appropriate. As they started to outgrow the whelping box, I put a playpen on the bathroom floor. Sitting inside it with them, I was able to supervise as they explored scary edges. At first they squirmed and huddled and meowed, afraid of their larger environment, but soon I became their jungle gym. Running up and down my arms, legs, and back, they tickled me, and I giggled when they tangled with my hair at the nape of my neck.

When they outgrew that space, I opened the bathroom door to the hallway and put up a furniture barricade. Every week I pushed out the bulwark to enhance their world little by little.

Eventually I lined the entire hall with giant towels and blankets. On top of that I put dozens of baskets and boxes for climbing or sleeping and strewed toys all over the place. I placed a tall carpet-covered cat tree on its side to turn it into a tiny-tot play structure. The kittens were hilarious, chasing, running, hiding, and pouncing as they wove in and out of the intricate obstacle course.

For hours each day and night, I sat on the floor participating in their antics. At naptime the kittens cuddled on my lap or stretched out on my long legs. When they nursed with their mother or snuggled with each other, I read a book or pondered how to share my sense of the sacred with a larger world.

That's when I birthed the idea to write a memoir and define my spiritual vocation. In perfect timing, when the kittens were ready to debut from the basement, I was finally feeling settled into our beautiful and perfectly organized ranch house.

But the second I reveled in my hard-earned and newfound freedom, life threw me a twist.

Both of our kids moved back home. Caught off guard, I nearly fainted. Ella, who had previously made plans to live with her friends after graduation, suddenly decided to save on rent. At the same time, Jake announced his plans to drop out of college because he was "uninspired by memorizing and regurgitating information."

Overnight, my simple, serene, and perfectly arranged smaller home had mountains of dirty clothes, shoes, boxes, and a myriad of stuff strewn all over the place with no empty cupboards, closets, or shelves to hide them. From that point forward, day in and day out, there was a nonstop flurry of action, questions, and disruptions of the peaceful flow I desperately tried to maintain.

As I began to write my book, I worked in the office I shared with Rhys. Surrounded by felines, I quickly understood that creative writing was an intuitive, holistic, right-brain activity that required me to relax and open in order to receive authentic inspiration from my muse. There was no way to force the results like I could as a high-tech professional, household manager, or school volunteer. In those roles, I used my analytical left brain to methodically break down the work into pieces in order to start, stop, multitask, or power through with sheer will when needed.

Often in the process of writing my life story, I was not typing at all. Instead I was sitting in my chair, staring at the wall, opening and closing my eyes, imagining, daydreaming, and talking to myself. Although those were some of my methods for receiving inspiration, it appeared that I was doing nothing of significance, which made me a sitting duck. Quite regularly one of my family members would pop in to chat, share their problems, ask for help, or invite me to join them in an activity.

One week when I was particularly busy with deadlines, I put up a warning by asking my family to pretend I had a nine-to-five job outside the home. I implored them to shift their perspective and said, "Please do not interrupt me during those hours." When small and big interferences continued to happen, I moved my workspace into the living room and shut the pocket door. When that did not work, I resorted to level three by taping a giant sign at the threshold that said, "Working all day to meet deadlines. Please do not disturb. Thank you."

Remarkably, Rhys opened the door without knocking and said, "Can you send a fax for me?" A year prior I would have reacted in a burst of heated emotions, tears, and complaints: "I have so much work to do. I'll never get it done. No one understands me." Blah, blah, blah. Instead I just looked up and calmly asked him, "Is it urgent?"

He said, "Well, no, but I want to send it soon."

I asked him if it had to go out that day. He said no.

Gently but firmly, I responded, "OK. I'll send it tomorrow." With a slightly perplexed look on his face, he shut the door.

It felt good to stand in my power with compassion amidst chaos. Finally there was no one to blame, and I was not a victim. Building on that confidence, I sent an e-mail to my very large extended family. Thanking them in advance for their support, I declared I would not be able to text, call, host, or visit them for several months. Without guilt, I cleared space to finish my book. Inwardly, I knew I had served my clan well and was ready to expand my family by embracing the world as my tribe and sharing the wisdom I had garnered.

The next day, I found a dead great horned owl who had been hit by a car. At home I took her out into the orchard and cradled her in my arms like a baby. Cherishing the soft touch of her caramel, cream, and brown feathers, I played with the tufts on her head. After naming her Buho, which is Spanish for owl, I sang her a lullaby. When I asked what she would like me to do with her body, she responded, *Please make me whole.*

Skinning, prepping, stuffing, and sewing Owl back together would be a very intimate process and symbolic of the journey to reclaim my full self. I had no formal taxidermy experience, but I decided to do it anyway.

In taxidermy it's not necessary to open the chest cavity. Once the animal is skinned, the body's flesh and bones are discarded whole. Of course I was compelled to go deep and found myself touching Owl's viscera. When I reached up into Buho's chest cavity, with no effort from me at all, her heart fell into the palm of my left hand. This had never happened to me before, and I gasped to see the vibrancy of Buho's love glistening red on my skin. Deeply touched, my eyes welled up with tears. Owl had confirmed I was walking the heart path.

About a month later, I learned it was a federal crime to possess any part of a raptor, including a feather. So I immediately buried Buho and her heart, returning them to the soil. At the same time, I was saddened to learn that California law prohibits the collection of road kill, native bird feathers, owl pellets, and other animal parts. Performing a second ceremony, I buried anything I had that was questionable.

For much of my life I suffered from a spiritual crisis because few knew me on the inside. Tamed and shamed, my sacred wild soul was starched, splintered, and scattered until bone by bone I pieced myself back together and fleshed myself out to become fully furred and wholly whole.

Realizing my authentic wildness in a civilized world has enlivened me. Free, spontaneous, and guided by the wisdom of my inner and outer natures, I am still able to coexist with a modern society.

Like Owl, I see in the dark. My wound was ultimately turned into a gift. Now it is my vocation to see, value, and encourage the hidden souls I see inside other people.

May my story inspire and guide you to remember your full self and shine your authentic wildness from the inside out.

heart to heart

I offer the deepest love and gratitude to these people.

My Mother and Father
I love you deeply in your fullness and am blessed to have you as my parents. I am grateful to have lived an extraordinary life and know I would not be the woman I am without you.

My Children
You are my greatest gifts and finest teachers. You bring me joy. Thank you for seeing and loving all of me. I love you deeply.

My Sisters
Thank you for being my blood sisters and female friends in the deepest, truest, circular ways of being. I love you deeply.

My Husband
Thank you for being my life partner, co-manifester, and solid platform. I love you deeply.

Eagle
Thank you for showing me how to love my full self. I love you deeply.

My Spiritual Teachers and Guides
Thank you for decades of inspiration and guidance as I peeled back and became immersed in deep layers of esoteric wisdom.

Dream Team

Thank you to this talented and heart-centric team:
Sal Borriello, Jan Johnson, Janis Monaco Clark, editors
Kathryn Hall and Antonia Hall, editors
Lindsy Richards, book-cover photographer
Bill Greaves, book-cover designer
Sara Zieve Miller, illustrator
Sal Borriello and Kevin Callahan, book production

CPSIA information can be obtained
at www.ICGtesting.com
Printed in the USA
FSHW01n1558200618
49603FS